Uncover 1

Combo A

Ben Goldstein • Ceri Jones

with Kathryn O'Dell

Student's Book

CB071276

CAMBRIDGE UNIVERSITY PRESS

Discovery EDUCATION

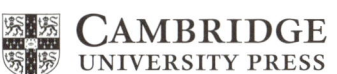

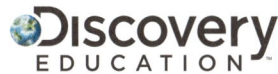

CAMBRIDGE
UNIVERSITY PRESS

University Printing House, Cambridge CB2 8BS, United Kingdom

One Liberty Plaza, 20th Floor, New York, NY 10006, USA

477 Williamstown Road, Port Melbourne, VIC 3207, Australia

314–321, 3rd Floor, Plot 3, Splendor Forum, Jasola District Centre, New Delhi – 110025, India

79 Anson Road, #06–04/06, Singapore 079906

Cambridge University Press is part of the University of Cambridge.

It furthers the University's mission by disseminating knowledge in the pursuit of education, learning and research at the highest international levels of excellence.

www.cambridge.org
Information on this title: www.cambridge.org/9781107514973

© Cambridge University Press 2015

This publication is in copyright. Subject to statutory exception and to the provisions of relevant collective licensing agreements, no reproduction of any part may take place without the written permission of Cambridge University Press.

First published 2015

20 19 18 17 16 15 14 13 12

Printed in Poland by Opolgraf

A catalog record for this publication is available from the British Library

ISBN 978-1-107-49302-5 Student's Book 1
ISBN 978-1-107-49303-2 Student's Book with Online Workbook and Online Practice 1
ISBN 978-1-107-51497-3 Combo 1A
ISBN 978-1-107-51501-7 Combo 1B
ISBN 978-1-107-49312-4 Teacher's Edition 1
ISBN 978-1-107-49307-0 Workbook with Online Practice 1
ISBN 978-1-107-49319-3 Presentation Plus Disc 1
ISBN 978-1-107-49313-1 Class Audio CDs (2) 1
ISBN 978-1-107-49314-8 Video DVD 1

Additional resources for this publication at www.cambridge.org/uncover

Cambridge University Press has no responsibility for the persistence or accuracy of URLs for external or third-party Internet websites referred to in this publication and does not guarantee that any content on such websites is, or will remain, accurate or appropriate. Information regarding prices, travel timetables, and other factual information given in this work is correct at the time of first printing but Cambridge University Press does not guarantee the accuracy of such information thereafter.

Art direction, book design, layout services, and photo research: QBS Learning
Audio production: John Marshall Media

Acknowledgments

Many teachers, coordinators, and educators shared their opinions, their ideas, and their experience to help create *Uncover*. The authors and publisher would like to thank the following people and their schools for their help in shaping the series.

In Mexico:

María Nieves Maldonado Ortiz (Colegio Enrique Rébsamen); Héctor Guzmán Pineda (Liceo Europeo); Alfredo Salas López (Campus Universitario Siglo XXI); Rosalba Millán Martínez (IIPAC [Instituto Torres Quintero A.C.]); Alejandra Rubí Reyes Badillo (ISAS [Instituto San Angel del Sur]); José Enrique Gutiérrez Escalante (Centro Escolar Zama); Gabriela Juárez Hernández (Instituto de Estudios Básicos Amado Nervo); Patricia Morelos Alonso (Instituto Cultural Ingles, S.C.); Martha Patricia Arzate Fernández, (Colegio Valladolid); Teresa González, Eva Marina Sánchez Vega (Colegio Salesiano); María Dolores León Ramírez de Arellano, (Liceo Emperadores Aztecas); Esperanza Medina Cruz (Centro Educativo Francisco Larroyo); Nubia Nelly Martínez García (Salesiano Domingo Savio); Diana Gabriela González Benítez (Colegio Ghandi); Juan Carlos Luna Olmedo (Centro Escolar Zama); Dulce María Pascual Granados (Esc. Juan Palomo Martínez); Roberto González, Fernanda Audirac (Real Life English Center); Rocio Licea (Escuela Fundación Mier y Pesado); Diana Pombo (Great Union Institute); Jacobo Cortés Vázquez (Instituto María P. de Alvarado); Michael John Pryor (Colegio Salesiano Anáhuac Chapalita)

In Brazil:

Renata Condi de Souza (Colégio Rio Branco); Sônia Maria Bernal Leites (Colégio Rio Branco); Élcio Souza (Centro Universitário Anhaguera de São Paulo); Patricia Helena Nero (Private teacher); Célia Elisa Alves de Magalhães (Colégio Cruzeiro-Jacarepaguá); Lilia Beatriz Freitas Gussem (Escola Parque-Gávea); Sandra Maki Kuchiki (Easy Way Idiomas); Lucia Maria Abrão Pereira Lima (Colégio Santa Cruz-São Paulo); Deborah de Castro Ferroz de Lima Pinto (Mundinho Segmento); Clara Vianna Prado (Private teacher); Ligia Maria Fernandes Diniz (Escola Internacional de Alphaville); Penha Aparecida Gaspar Rodrigues (Colégio Salesiano Santa Teresinha); Silvia Castelan (Colégio Santa Catarina de Sena); Marcelo D'Elia (The Kids Club Guarulhos); Malyina Kazue Ono Leal (Colégio Bandeirantes); Nelma de Mattos Santana Alves (Private teacher); Mariana Martins Machado (Britannia Cultural); Lilian Bluvol Vaisman (Curso Oxford); Marcelle Belfort Duarte (Cultura Inglesa-Duque de Caxias); Paulo Dantas (Britannia International English); Anauã Carmo Vilhena (York Language Institute); Michele Amorim Estellita (Lemec – Lassance Modern English Course); Aida Setton (Colégio Uirapuru); Maria Lucia Zaorob (CEL-LEP); Marisa Veiga Lobato (Interlíngua Idiomas); Maria Virgínia Lebrón (Independent consultant); Maria Luiza Carmo (Colégio Guilherme Dumont Villares/CEL-LEP); Lucia Lima (Independent consultant); Malyina Kazue Ono Leal (Colégio Bandeirantes); Debora Schisler (Seven Idiomas); Helena Nagano (Cultura Inglesa); Alessandra de Campos (Alumni); Maria Lúcia Sciamarelli (Colégio Divina Providência); Catarina Kruppa (Cultura Inglesa); Roberto Costa (Freelance teacher/consultant); Patricia McKay Aronis (CEL-LEP); Claudia Beatriz Cavalieri (By the World Idiomas); Sérgio Lima (Vermont English School); Rita Miranda (IBI – [Instituto Batista de Idiomas]); Maria de Fátima Galery (Britain English School); Marlene Almeida (Teacher Trainer Consultant); Flávia Samarane (Colégio Logosófico); Maria Tereza Vianna (Greenwich Schools); Daniele Brauer (Cultura Inglesa/AMS Idiomas); Allessandra Cierno (Colégio Santa Dorotira); Helga Silva Nelken (Greenwich Schools/Colégio Edna Roriz); Regina Marta Bazzoni (Britain English School); Adriano Reis (Greenwich Schools); Vanessa Silva Freire de Andrade (Private teacher); Nilvane Guimarães (Colégio Santo Agostinho)

In Ecuador:

Santiago Proaño (Independent teacher trainer); Tania Abad (UDLA [Universidad de Las Americas]); Rosario Llerena (Colegio Isaac Newton); Paúl Viteri (Colegio Andino); Diego Maldonado (Central University); Verónica Vera (Colegio Tomás Moro); Mónica Sarauz (Colegio San Gabriel); Carolina Flores (Colegio APCH); Boris Cadena, Vinicio Reyes (Colegio Benalcázar); Deigo Ponce (Colegio Gonzaga); Byron Freire (Colegio Nuestra Señora del Rosario)

The authors and publisher would also like to thank the following contributors, script writers, and collaborators for their inspired work in creating *Uncover*:
Anna Whitcher, Janet Gokay, Kathryn O'Dell, Lynne Robertson, and Dana Henricks

Unit	Vocabulary	Grammar	Listening	Conversation (Useful language)
1 Welcome Back! pp. 2–11	- Classroom objects - Colors - Instructions	- Simple present of *be* - Subject pronouns - Imperatives Grammar reference p. 106	- Important announcements	- Learning a new language
2 My World pp. 12–21	- Personal items - Countries, nationalities, languages	- Possessive adjectives, *'s, s'* - Question words Grammar reference p. 107	- Making new friends	- Meeting and greeting
3 People in My Life pp. 22–31	- Family and friends - Describing people	- *have* - Comparative adjectives - Possessive pronouns Grammar reference p. 108	- A computer game	- On the phone
4 It's My Life! pp. 32–41	- Daily routines - After-school activities	- Simple present statements - Simple present questions - Adverbs of frequency Grammar reference p. 109	- Podcast interviews about after-school activities	- Asking for information
5 School Days pp. 42–51	- Places at school - School subjects	- *can* for ability - Object pronouns - Verb + *-ing* form (gerund) for opinions Grammar reference p. 110	- A student's experience at a performing arts school	- Asking for and giving permission

Unit 1–5 Review Game pp. 52–53

Writing	Reading	Video	Accuracy and fluency	Speaking outcomes
■ A poster with classroom rules	■ *It's a New School Year* ■ Reading to write: *Computer Club Rules* ■ Culture: *Picture It!*	■ *Anuj's First Day* ■ *How do you spell your name?* ■ *Zhin Yan: A Gymnast*	■ *a* vs. *an* ■ Rising intonation in *yes/no* questions ■ Singular form of *be* for groups	I can . . . ■ identify classroom objects and colors. ■ identify people in my school. ■ give and follow instructions. ■ ask for help learning English. ■ talk about a school club.
■ A personal profile	■ *Jessica Watson – A Teenage Sailor!* ■ Reading to write: *Meet the Team* ■ Culture: *Our World in a Box*	■ *The Yellow Ferrari* ■ *What's your name? Where are you from?* ■ *Young Scientists* ■ *The Land Down Under* (CLIL Project p. 116)	■ Using demonstratives *this, that, these,* and *those* in introductions ■ Falling intonation in *Wh-* questions ■ Capital letters with countries, nationalities, and languages ■ Conjugation of *be* after plural possessives	I can . . . ■ identify personal items. ■ talk about my favorite things. ■ ask and answer questions about people's background and nationality. ■ meet, greet, and introduce people. ■ choose things for a time capsule.
■ A description of a person	■ *A Very Big Family!* ■ Reading to write: *My Best Friend* ■ Culture: *Diwali*	■ *Robot Fighters* ■ *What's your phone number? What's your email address?* ■ *My Siberian Family*	■ Using *It's . . .* to identify yourself on the phone ■ Word stress with comparative adjectives ■ Not using *more* with comparative adjectives ending in *-er*	I can . . . ■ identify my family members and friends. ■ talk about my family. ■ compare people. ■ talk on the phone. ■ talk about festivals.
■ A blog post about your routine	■ *Times Around the World* ■ Reading to write: *Madison's Blog* ■ Culture: *It's a New Year!*	■ *Ali's Day* ■ *What do you do after school?* ■ *La Quinceañera* ■ *Mars* (CLIL Project p. 117)	■ Irregular spellings of third person simple present form ■ Different sounds of third person simple present forms: /s/, /z/, /iz/ ■ Position of adverbs of frequency	I can . . . ■ talk about my daily routine. ■ talk about things I do and don't do. ■ ask and answer questions about routines and activities. ■ ask questions for more information. ■ discuss a special occasion.
■ An email asking for permission	■ *Kung Fu School* ■ Reading to write: *Using the Computer Lab* ■ Culture: *A Do-It-Yourself School*	■ *Kung Fu School* ■ *Can you use your cell phone at school?* ■ *Tobilay's School Day*	■ Different vowel sounds for *can* and *can't* ■ *Well* vs. *good*	I can . . . ■ identify places at my school. ■ talk about my abilities. ■ express opinions about school subjects and activities. ■ ask for and give permission. ■ discuss interesting or unusual things about schools.

1 Welcome BACK!

Discovery EDUCATION
BE CURIOUS

- Anuj's First Day
- How do you spell your name?
- Jin Yang: A Gymnast

1. How many people are in the photo?
2. Who are they?
3. Where are they?

UNIT CONTENTS

Vocabulary Classroom objects and colors; instructions
Grammar Simple present of *be* and subject pronouns; imperatives
Listening Important announcements

Vocabulary: Classroom objects and colors

1. Match the words with the correct items.

1. _k_ a backpack
2. ___ a board
3. ___ a book
4. ___ a bookshelf
5. ___ a chair
6. ___ a desk
7. ___ a dictionary
8. ___ a notebook
9. ___ a pencil
10. ___ a ruler
11. ___ an eraser

 2. Listen, check, and repeat.

3. Look at the picture in Exercise 1. Write the colors of the classroom objects.

1. a __black__ chair
2. a _____ bookshelf
3. a _____ desk
4. a _____ book
5. a _____ eraser
6. a _____ notebook
7. a _____ dictionary
8. a _____ board
9. a _____ backpack
10. a _____ pencil
11. an _____ ruler

> **NOTICE IT**
> Use **a** before a word that starts with a consonant. Use **an** before a word that starts with a vowel or vowel sound.
> **a c**hair **an e**raser
> **a r**uler **an o**range ruler

 4. Listen, check, and repeat.

Speaking: My classroom objects

5. Check (✓) the items that are in your desk or your backpack. Add another item.

- ☐ a laptop
- ☐ a book
- ☐ an eraser
- ☐ a notebook
- ☐ a dictionary
- ☐ a pencil
- ☐ a ruler
- ☐ Other: _____

6. YOUR TURN Work with a partner. Say the items in your desk or backpack and their colors.

> A yellow and gray book, an orange eraser, . . .

> Workbook, p. 2

Reading It's a New School Year; Computer Club Rules; Picture It!
Conversation Learning a new language
Writing A poster with classroom rules

Unit 1 | 3

It's a NEW SCHOOL YEAR!

Reading: Notices on a bulletin board

1. Look at the pictures. What is the calendar about?

2. Read and listen to the notices. Circle the best title.
   a. People at Clinton Middle School!
   b. This Week at Clinton Middle School!
   c. Football Is Now for Boys and Girls!

3. Read the notices again. Complete the chart with the times and places.

Event	Time	Place
1. ice cream party	after lunch	
2. NexGen Inventors' Club meeting		
3. girls' football team tryouts		
4. school website meeting		
5. rock band contest		

4. **YOUR TURN** Work with a partner. Make a list of activities at your school. Then say your favorite activities.

   Boys and girls soccer, a science club, a dance group, . . .

4 | Unit 1

Grammar: Simple present of *be* and subject pronouns

5. Complete the chart.

Use the simple present of *be* to identify people and give locations and dates. Subject pronouns can replace the names of the people or things that the sentences are about.

Affirmative	Negative
I am a photographer.	**I am not** a musician.
Laura _____ 12 years old.	**She is not** 13 years old.
Tryouts **are** on the football field.	**They** _____ in the gym.

Yes/No questions	Short answers
Are you a photographer?	Yes, **I** _____. No, **I'm not**.
_____ Laura 12 years old?	Yes, **she is**. No, **she isn't**.
Are tryouts on the football field?	Yes, **they** _____. No, **they aren't**.

Subject pronoun	I		you	he	she		it	we	they
Simple present of *be*	_____		are	is		_____	is	are	_____

> Check your answers: Grammar reference, p. 106

Get it RIGHT!
Use the singular form of *be* for nouns that represent groups of people.
The band **is** good.
NOT: ~~The band **are** good.~~
The team **is** all girls.
NOT: ~~The team **are** all girls.~~

6. Complete the sentences with the simple present forms of *be*.

1. The ruler ___is___ gray.
2. Kyle and Leila _____ photographers.
3. You _____ in my class.
4. I _____ a football player.
5. The band _____ new.
6. The meetings _____ on Thursdays.

7. Make the sentences in Exercise 6 negative. Use contractions.

1. *The ruler isn't yellow.*
2. _____
3. _____
4. _____
5. _____
6. _____

8. Write *yes/no* questions with the simple present forms of *be*.

1. you / 12 years old *Are you 12 years old?*
2. you / a teacher _____
3. your friends / in a band _____
4. your school / big _____

Say it RIGHT!
The voice rises in *yes/no* questions. Listen and repeat the questions in Exercise 8.
Are you 12 years old? ⬆
Ask and answer the questions in Exercise 8 with a partner. Make sure your voice rises when you ask the questions.

Speaking: It's not true!

9. YOUR TURN Write three false sentences about you or people in your school.

1. *I'm 15 years old*
2. *Mrs. King is an English teacher.*
3. *Tim is in a band.*

10. Work with a partner. Share your sentences. Ask and answer questions to correct them.

> OK. You aren't 15 years old. Are you 12 years old?
>> No, I'm not.
> Are you 11?
>> Yes, I am.

BE CURIOUS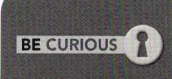
Find out about Anuj and his school. Why is it a special day? (Workbook p. 72)

1.1 ANUJ'S FIRST DAY

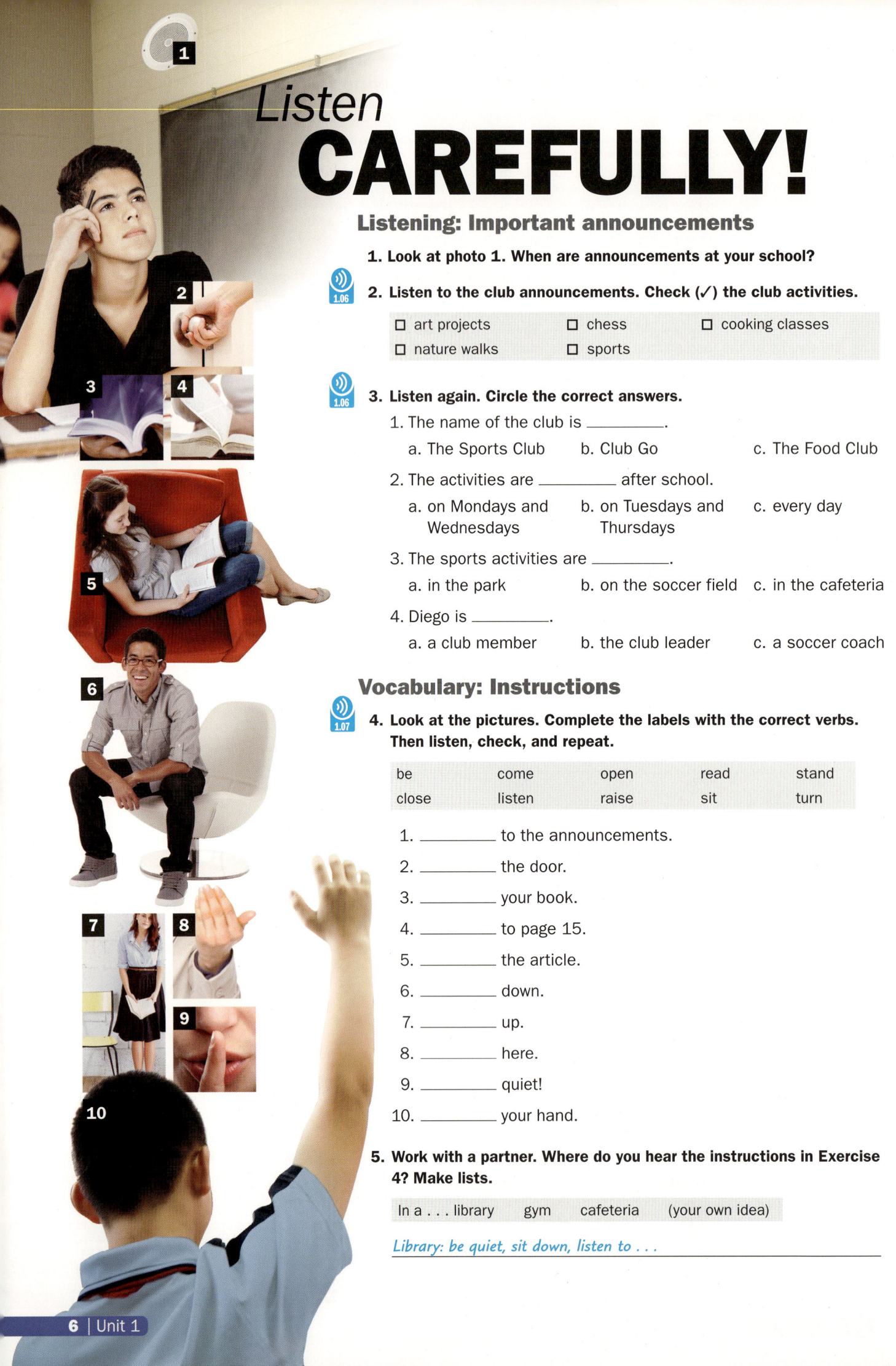

Listen CAREFULLY!

Listening: Important announcements

1. Look at photo 1. When are announcements at your school?

2. Listen to the club announcements. Check (✓) the club activities.

   ☐ art projects   ☐ chess   ☐ cooking classes
   ☐ nature walks   ☐ sports

3. Listen again. Circle the correct answers.

   1. The name of the club is _____.
      a. The Sports Club   b. Club Go   c. The Food Club
   2. The activities are _____ after school.
      a. on Mondays and Wednesdays   b. on Tuesdays and Thursdays   c. every day
   3. The sports activities are _____.
      a. in the park   b. on the soccer field   c. in the cafeteria
   4. Diego is _____.
      a. a club member   b. the club leader   c. a soccer coach

Vocabulary: Instructions

4. Look at the pictures. Complete the labels with the correct verbs. Then listen, check, and repeat.

be	come	open	read	stand
close	listen	raise	sit	turn

   1. _____ to the announcements.
   2. _____ the door.
   3. _____ your book.
   4. _____ to page 15.
   5. _____ the article.
   6. _____ down.
   7. _____ up.
   8. _____ here.
   9. _____ quiet!
   10. _____ your hand.

5. Work with a partner. Where do you hear the instructions in Exercise 4? Make lists.

   In a . . . library   gym   cafeteria   (your own idea)

   Library: be quiet, sit down, listen to . . .

6 | Unit 1

Grammar: Imperatives

6. Complete the chart.

Use imperatives to give commands or instructions.	
Affirmative	**Negative**
Close the door.	**Don't close** the door.
Turn to page 7.	_____ turn to page 8.
_____ on the soccer field.	**Don't meet** in the gym.
Contraction do not = _____	

 Check your answers: Grammar reference, p. 106

7. Match the phrases.

1. Be
2. Please turn
3. Write
4. Don't look
5. Don't listen
6. Ask the teacher

a. for help.
b. at the answers.
c. your name on your paper, please.
d. to music on your phone.
e. on time for class, please.
f. to page 6 in your book.

NOTICE IT
Use **please** to make a command softer. It can go at the beginning or end of a sentence. Use a comma before **please** when it goes at the end of a sentence.
Please listen carefully.
Listen carefully, **please**.
Please don't open your books.
Don't open your books, **please**.

8. Look at the classroom rules. Write imperative sentences with please.

CLASSROOM RULES

DO	DON'T
1. read the rules	4. run in the classroom
2. raise your hand	5. talk on the phone
3. listen carefully	6. sit on your desk

1. *Please read the rules.*
2. _____
3. _____
4. _____
5. _____
6. _____

Speaking: Do it! Don't do it!

9. YOUR TURN Work with a partner. Give instructions. Your partner does the actions. Take turns.

Workbook, pp. 4–5

REAL TALK 1.2 HOW DO YOU SPELL YOUR NAME?

What does rule MEAN?

Conversation: That's my name!

 1. **REAL TALK** Watch or listen to the teenagers. Complete their names with the correct letters.

1. E-____-I-____-Y
2. P-E-____-____-A
3. ____-A-____-H-E-L ____-A-N-____
4. ____-O-____-____-T-____-E-____
5. E-____-____-N
6. ____-____-N-N-____
7. ____-____-E-____-E-N
8. ____-R-E-D-D-____-____

2. **YOUR TURN** How do you spell *your* name? Tell your partner.

3. Listen to Cesar and Leah. Complete the conversation.

USEFUL LANGUAGE: Learning a new language
Can you repeat that · How do you say · I don't understand · What does . . . mean

Leah: Hi, **Cesar**.

Cesar: Hey, **Leah**. Look at this cool notebook. It's for new English words.

Leah: Nice.

Cesar: ¹_____ *regla* in English?

Leah: Ruler.

Cesar: I'm sorry. ²_____. How do you spell it?

Leah: **R-U-L-E-R**.

Cesar: ³_____, please?

Leah: Sure, it's **R-U-L-E-R**.

Cesar: Oh, **ruler**. Thanks. Here's a new word for me, too . . . rule. ⁴_____ rule _____?

Leah: Rules are things you can and can't do . . . you know, like *listen to the teacher* and *don't use your phone in class*!

Cesar: I see. Thanks!

4. Practice the conversation with a partner.

5. **YOUR TURN** Repeat the conversation in Exercise 3, but change the words in **purple**. Use your own names, the items below, and the words for them in your first language.

a marker · a pen · a calculator · a map · _____ (your own idea)

Computer Club Rules

1. Be on time! Club meetings are at 4:00 on Mondays.
2. Be careful with the laptops. They are new.
3. Please be quiet in the lab. Use headphones.
4. Don't eat or drink in the computer lab.
5. Please take turns.
6. Don't sit on the desks!
7. Don't use phones in the lab.
8. Turn off the computers at the end of the day.

Reading to write: A poster with classroom rules

6. Look at the title and pictures on the poster. What do you think some of the rules are? Read the poster to check.

> **Focus on CONTENT**
> A list of rules can include examples of things to *do* and things *not* to do.

7. Read each rule below. Write the number of the rule in the poster that means the same thing.

   1. Don't be late. ___
   2. Don't talk loudly in the lab. ___
   3. Sit on the chairs. ___
   4. Turn your phones off. ___
   5. Don't leave the computers on. ___

> **Focus on LANGUAGE**
> **Exclamation points**
> Use an exclamation point to show something is:
> - very important: *Listen carefully!*
> - dangerous: *Don't sit on the table!* (It might break.)
> Don't use too many exclamation points.

8. Find the rules in the poster with exclamation points. Which one shows something is very important? Which one shows something is dangerous?

9. Add missing periods or exclamation points to the sentences.

   1. Don't talk in the library___ It's very important.
   2. Help me with my homework, please___
   3. Don't run in the hallway___ You might fall.
   4. The English class is at 10:00___

Writing: Classroom rules

PLAN
Make a chart with ideas for classroom rules. Then number your ideas in the order of importance.

Do	Don't

WRITE
Now write your rules. Use the best ideas in your chart. Write at least eight rules.

CHECK
Check your writing. Can you answer "yes" to these questions?

- Do you include things to *do* and things *not* to do?
- Do you use exclamation points correctly?

PICTURE IT!

NYC SALT is an after-school photography program in New York City. The students are 13 to 19 years old. The teens' photos are about their interests and cultures. The classes are one day a week.

Here's a list of things you do at NYC SALT:
- Learn about your camera.
- Learn from professional photographers.
- Use your camera on photo shoots.
- Show your photos in the SALT gallery.
- Make videos.
- Become an artist!

Some teens are part of group projects. For example, *Life in Washington Heights* is a collection of photos about a neighborhood in New York City. The photos are on the streets and in the parks in Washington Heights. The photos are also in the photographers' homes, on subways, and in supermarkets. Some photos are black and white, and others are in color.

Are you a photographer? Is there an after-school program in your city?

YES ☐ *Join today!*

NO ☐ *Start your own photography club!*

Culture: Student photographers

1. **Look at the title and pictures. What is the article about? Check (✓) your guess.**
   - ☐ professional photographers in New York City
   - ☐ a photography program in New York City
   - ☐ teens in New York City

2. **Read and listen to the article. Check your answer in Exercise 1.** (1.10)

3. **Read the article again. Circle the correct answers.**
   1. The **teachers / students** at NYC SALT are teens.
   2. The students' photos are about their **interests and cultures / schools and teachers**.
   3. The classes are **one / five** day(s) a week.
   4. Students learn how to use **cameras / computers** in the program.
   5. *Life in Washington Heights* is a **photography / video** project.

4. **YOUR TURN** Work with a partner. Talk about a club that *you* are in or a club that you know about.

   > Are you in a club?

   > Yes, I am. I'm in a music club. It's on Mondays, and it's in the band room. It's fun. It . . .

DID YOU KNOW…?
First black and white photo: 1826
First color photo: 1861
First digital camera: 1975

BE CURIOUS Find out about Jin Yang, a gymnast. Where is her school? (Workbook, p. 73)

Discovery EDUCATION

1.3 JIN YANG: A GYMNAST

UNIT 1 REVIEW

Vocabulary

1. Write a/an, the color, and the classroom object.

1. _____
2. _____
3. _____
4. _____

2. Put the sentences in the most logical order.

____ Close your book.

____ Open your book.

_1_ Sit down in your chair.

____ Read the article.

____ Turn to page 13.

Grammar

3. Write sentences with the simple present forms of *be*. Use subject pronouns for names and objects. Use contractions.

1. Amy / not 17 / .

   She's not 17. / She isn't 17.

2. Paula and Rico / in an English club / .

   _____

3. the chair / not / green / .

   _____

4. the rulers / yellow / ?

   _____

4. Write the negative form of the imperative sentences.

1. Run in the gym.

   _____

2. Come here.

   _____

3. Please ask questions.

   _____

4. Raise your hand.

   _____

5. Stand up now.

   _____

6. Talk to your classmates.

   _____

Useful language

5. Circle the correct answers.

Hiro: Hello, Mika.

Mika: Morning, Hiro.

Hiro: (1) **How / What** do you say *sensei* in English?

Mika: Teacher.

Hiro: I don't (2) **mean / understand**. How do you spell it?

Mika: T-E-A-C-H-E-R.

Hiro: Can you (3) **repeat / say** that, please?

Mika: Sure. T-E-A-C-H-E-R.

Hiro: Oh, teacher. Thanks.

Mika: Hey, Hiro. What does *dictionary* (4) **say / mean**?

Hiro: Oh, I know that word. It's a book with words in it.

Mika: Yes! Buy a dictionary, please!

PROGRESS CHECK: Now I can . . .

☐ identify classroom objects and colors.

☐ identify people in my school.

☐ give and follow instructions.

☐ ask for help learning English.

☐ write a list of rules.

☐ talk about a school club.

2 My WORLD

Discovery EDUCATION

BE CURIOUS

The Yellow Ferrari

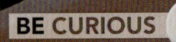
What's your name? Where are you from?

Young Scientists

The Land Down Under

1. Where is this?
2. What countries and ocean can you see?
3. Is your favorite place in the photo? Where is your favorite place?

UNIT CONTENTS

Vocabulary Personal items; countries, nationalities, and languages
Grammar Possessives; question words
Listening Making new friends

Vocabulary: Personal items

1. Label the pictures with the correct words.

   - ☐ a cell phone
   - ☐ a guitar
   - ☐ a skateboard
   - ☐ comic books
   - ☐ headphones
   - ☐ sneakers / tennis shoes
   - ☐ a computer / a laptop
   - ☐ inline skates
   - ☐ a soccer ball
   - ☑ a game console
   - ☐ an MP3 player
   - ☐ a tablet

1. *a game console*
2. _____
3. _____
4. _____
5. _____
6. _____
7. _____
8. _____
9. _____
10. _____
11. _____
12. _____

 2. Listen, check, and repeat.

3. Work with a partner. Put the personal items in the correct categories. Some items can go in more than one category.

Music	Technology	School	Sports	Reading
a guitar				

Speaking: Is it a . . . ?

4. **YOUR TURN** Describe a personal item from Exercise 1 to your partner, but don't say what it is! Your partner guesses it. Take turns.

   > It's black and white. It's for a sport.
   >
   > Is it a soccer ball?
   >
   > Yes, it is.

5. Work with a different partner. Repeat Exercise 4. How many items can you guess correctly in five minutes?

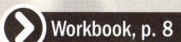 Workbook, p. 8

Reading Jessica Watson – A Teenage Sailor!; Meet the Team; Our World in a Box
Conversation Meeting and greeting
Writing A personal profile

Favorite THINGS

FACT FILE
NAME: Jessica Watson
NATIONALITY: Australian
RECORD: The first teenager to sail around the world alone.

Jessica Watson – A Teenage Sailor!

This is Jessica Watson. She's Australian, and she's 16. She's a sailor. The ocean is her favorite place, and her boat is her favorite thing. Pink is her favorite color. Of course, her boat is pink! Its name is *Pink Lady*.

Jessica is on the *Pink Lady*. She's on a trip around the world from Sydney Harbour in Australia, over the Pacific, Atlantic, and Indian Oceans, and back to Sydney. That's 23,000 miles! She's on the Indian Ocean now.

Jessica's friends and family are at home in Australia. She speaks to her mother and father every day on her satellite phone. Her satellite phone is very important. It's her connection with her family – and the world.

Reading: An article about a teen adventurer

1. Look at the title, photos, and fact file. Who is the article about? Why is she famous?

2. Read and listen to the article. What is Jessica's favorite place? Her favorite thing? Her favorite color?

3. Read the article again. Correct the sentences.

   1. Jessica is from the United States. *Jessica is from Australia.*
   2. Jessica is in her house now. _____
   3. The *Pink Lady* is on the Atlantic Ocean. _____
   4. Her mother and father are on the boat. _____
   5. She speaks to her friends every day. _____

4. **YOUR TURN** Pretend you are on a trip. Think of ideas and complete the chart. Then tell your partner.

Name of your boat	
Places on your trip	
People on your trip	

> My boat is the *Blue Whale*. I'm on a trip from Australia to India. I'm with my friend Benny and . . . .

Grammar: Possessives

5. Complete the chart.

Use a possessive adjective or a name/noun + 's to show possession. For plural subjects, add s'.								
Subject pronouns	I	you	he	she	it	we	you	they
Possessive adjectives	my **Her** boat is pink.	your	his	_____ name is *Pink Lady*.	its	our	your	their
Possessive 's or s'	Jessica _____ boat is pink. The **boat's** name is *Pink Lady*. The **boats'** names are *Blue Whale* and *Pink Lady*.							

> Check your answers: Grammar reference, p. 107

6. Underline the possessive adjectives.

Hi, I'm Doug. My favorite thing is my skateboard. My friend is Lucy. Her favorite thing is her bike. Look at our dogs. Their names are Zack and Blackie. My dog is Blackie. His favorite thing is this blue ball.

7. Circle the correct answers.

This is me and (1) **my / your** friends. We're on (2) **its / our** skateboards. My skateboard is a gift from (3) **our / my** parents. Look at David and (4) **his / her** green skateboard. He's (5) **my / his** best friend. Look at Laura and (6) **his / her** best friend Maria. They're fast! We're all good at skateboarding! What's (7) **your / you** favorite sport?

8. Write sentences with possessive 's or s'.

1. Marcy / bike / green — *Marcy's bike is green.*
2. Jake / computer / new
3. Our parents / car / black
4. My dog / ball / small
5. Tom / comic books / old
6. My dogs / names / Spot and Luke

Get it RIGHT!

The **students'** names **are** Kyle and Sandy. = There is more than one student and more than one name.

The **students'** favorite class **is** English. = There is more than one student, but only one class.

Speaking: My list of favorites

9. YOUR TURN Complete the chart with your own information.

My favorite color	
My favorite game	
My favorite movie	
My favorite place	

10. Work with a partner. Talk about your favorite things.

> My favorite color is purple. My favorite game is . . .

11. Join another pair. Tell them about your partner's favorite things.

> Ian's favorite color is purple. His favorite game is . . .

BE CURIOUS Find out about this yellow Ferrari. Whose is it? (Workbook p. 74)

Discovery EDUCATION
2.1 THE YELLOW FERRARI

Where are YOU FROM?

Listening: Making new friends

1. Who are your friends? Where are they from?

2. Listen to three boys talking. Are Sam and Mateo friends?

3. Listen again. Circle the correct answers.

   1. It's _____.
      a. Sam's ball   b. Mateo's ball
   2. Mateo is _____.
      a. 14   b. 12
   3. Jack is _____.
      a. Mateo's friend   b. Sam's friend
   4. Jack is _____.
      a. 14   b. 12

Vocabulary: Countries, nationalities, and languages

4. Complete the chart with the correct nationalities and languages. Then listen, check, and repeat.

> **Get it RIGHT!**
> Use capital letters with countries, nationalities, and languages.
> *Spain* (NOT: *spain*)

☐ American ☐ Colombian ☐ Mexican
☐ Brazilian ☑ English ☐ Spanish
☐ British ☐ Italian ☐ Sudanese
☐ Canadian ☐ Japanese

Country	Nationality	Main Official Language(s)
Australia	Australian	(1) English
Brazil	(2)	Portuguese
Canada	(3)	English and French
Colombia	(4)	Spanish
Sudan	(5)	Arabic and English
Italy	Italian	(6)
Japan	Japanese	(7)
Mexico	(8)	Spanish
Spain	Spanish	(9)
the UK (the United Kingdom)	(10)	English
the US (the United States)	(11)	English

5. Work with a partner. Say the names, nationalities, and languages of people you know or famous people from the countries in Exercise 4. Take turns.

> Kaka is from Brazil. He's Brazilian. He speaks Portuguese.

Grammar: Question words

6. Complete the chart.

Use Wh- questions to ask about specific information.

Questions	Answers
_____ are you from?	Canada.
What _____ your favorite thing?	My guitar.
_____ old are you?	12.
Who _____ your classmates?	Felipe and Rachel.
When is your birthday?	September 21.

> Check your answers: Grammar reference, p. 107

7. Match the questions with the answers.

1. What's your favorite thing?
2. Who's your teacher?
3. How old are you?
4. Where are you from?
5. When are your Spanish classes?

a. I'm from Mexico.
b. I'm 14.
c. My skateboard.
d. On Tuesdays and Thursdays.
e. Mr. Simpson.

8. Complete the questionnaire with the correct question words.

1. *What* 's your name? Min-hee Ryu.
2. _____ are you? 13.
3. _____ are you from? South Korea.
4. _____ class are you in? English 202.
5. _____ is your teacher? Ms. Wilson.
6. _____ 's your teacher from? Australia.
7. _____ is your English class? At 3:00 on Thursdays.
8. _____ 's your favorite thing about class? Pair work.

Speaking: Who are you?

9. **YOUR TURN** Work with a partner. Put the words in the correct order to make questions. Then ask and answer the questions.

1. name / what's / your / ?   *What's your name?*
2. are / where / from / you / ? _____
3. you / are / old / how / ?   _____
4. birthday / when / your / is / ? _____
5. friends / your / are / who / ? _____
6. English class / your / when / is / ? _____

> What's your name?
>> Maria Salazar.

10. Work with a different partner. Ask and answer the questions about your partner from Exercise 9.

> What's your partner's name?
>> Samir Abdul.

 Say it RIGHT!

The voice rises in *yes/no* questions but falls in *Wh-* questions. Listen and repeat the questions.
Are you 15 years old? ↑
What's your name? ↓
Make sure your voice falls when you ask the questions in Exercises 9 and 10.

> Workbook, pp. 10–11

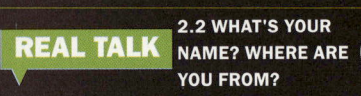 **REAL TALK** 2.2 WHAT'S YOUR NAME? WHERE ARE YOU FROM?

Nice to MEET YOU!

Conversation: Who's that over there?

1. **REAL TALK** Watch or listen to the teenagers. Match the names with the sentences.

   1. Rachel __c__
   2. Binny ____
   3. Steven ____
   4. Emily ____
   5. Courtney ____
   6. Freddie ____

   a. He's American, and his dad is Israeli.
   b. She's from the US, and her parents are from China.
   c. She's British, and she's from England.
   d. He's English, and his parents are from England.
   e. He's from the UK.
   f. She's from the UK, and her mom is from California.

2. **YOUR TURN** What's *your* name? Where are *you* from? Tell your partner.

3. Listen to Paola and Jen meeting each other for the first time. Complete the conversation.

USEFUL LANGUAGE: Meeting and greeting
Nice to meet you. | That's | This is | What about you?

Paola:	Hi. Are you on the **volleyball** team?
Jen:	Yes, I am. I'm **Jen**. What's your name?
Paola:	I'm **Paola**. I'm on the team, too.
Jen:	Cool! ¹_____ my friend **Liv**. She's also on the team.
Paola:	Hi, **Liv**.
Liv:	Hello, **Paola**. ²_____
Paola:	You, too. Hey, who's that over there?
Jen:	³_____ **Carla**. She's really good at **volleyball**!
Paola:	Where's **she** from?
Liv:	She's from **Colombia**. ⁴_____ Where are you from?
Paola:	I'm **Colombian**, too!

4. Practice the conversation in groups of three.

5. **YOUR TURN** Repeat the conversation in Exercise 3, but change the words in purple. Use the information in the chart.

Sport	Person over there	Country
basketball	David	Brazil
gymnastics	Wendy	Australia
baseball	Ken	Japan
(your own idea)	_____	_____

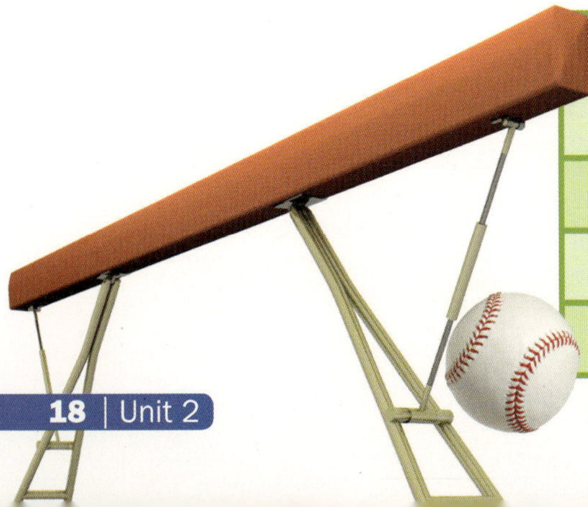

NOTICE IT
Use *this* and *these* to introduce people near you.
This is my friend Sue.
These are her parents, Mr. and Mrs. Cullen.
Use *that* or *those* to identify people who are far away.
That's my dad over there, and **those** are his friends.

18 | Unit 2

Meet the Team
PROFILES

My name's Hiroto Itou. I'm 12. My birthday's on March 13. This year it's on a Saturday! I'm Japanese, and I'm from Sapporo. My dad's from Japan, and my mom's from the United States. I speak Japanese and English.

My favorite music is hip-hop. My favorite sport is basketball, and my favorite team is the New York Knicks. My Knicks shirt is my favorite thing. My favorite colors are orange and blue. Those are the New York Knicks's colors!

Reading to write: A personal profile

6. Look at the photo in Hiroto's profile. What's his favorite sport? Read the profile to check.

   ◉ *Focus on* **CONTENT**
   A personal profile can include this information:
   name   age   birthday   nationality
   town / city   country   language(s)
   interests / favorite things

7. Read the profile again. Find Hiroto's information for each category in the Focus on Content box.

   ◉ *Focus on* **LANGUAGE**
   Capital letters
   Use capital letters
   - to start a sentence or question: **M**y class is . . . , **W**hen's your . . . ?
   - with names for people and teams: **J**en, the **T**igers
   - with towns/cities, countries, nationalities, and languages: **Q**uito, **I**taly, **C**anadian, **K**orean
   - with months and days: **F**ebruary, **M**onday

8. Find examples of each use of capital letters in the profile in Exercise 6.

9. Correct the sentences.
   1. I live in seoul.
      I live in Seoul.
   2. my birthday is on monday, december 6.
   3. I speak spanish and french.
   4. my favorite city is toronto.
   5. this is my friend larry.

 Writing: Your profile

◯ **PLAN**
Complete the chart with your own information.

Name	
Age	
Birthday	
Nationality	
Town / city	
Country	
Language(s)	
Favorite things	

◯ **WRITE**
Now write your personal profile. Use your chart to help you. Write at least 60 words.

◯ **CHECK**
Check your writing. Can you answer "yes" to these questions?

- Is information for each category from the Focus on Content box in your profile?
- Are the capital letters correct?

OUR WORLD IN A BOX

What is a time capsule? A time capsule is a box with different things in it. The things are from your life and culture today. Open your time capsule in the future, and see your life from the past! It's easy to make a time capsule.

1. Put important things from your life and culture in the box. Some ideas are favorite things, photos, music, and clothes.
2. Close the box. Choose a date and write it on the box. For example, "Open in 2050."
3. Find a place for the box. Don't open it for many years.
4. Open your time capsule on the date – or leave the time capsule for others to open.

Look at two time capsules from schools in the United States.

School:	Lyme-Old Lime High School	Fenway High School
City, State:	Lyme, Connecticut	Boston, Massachusetts
Objects:	■ a cell phone ■ photos ■ a school T-shirt ■ a school newspaper ■ an e-book ■ an American flag	■ a game console ■ photos ■ a school T-shirt ■ newspapers ■ a list of popular words ■ maps
Date to Open:	2046	2036

Now, make your own time capsule. It's easy and fun!

Culture: Time capsules

1. Look at the title and pictures. What does the title mean?

2. 🔊 2.08 Read and listen to the article. Check (✓) the things that are in the students' time capsules.

   ☐ art   ☐ photos
   ☐ clothes   ☐ technology
   ☐ music

3. Read the article again. Number the steps in the correct order.

   ____ Put your favorite things in the box.
   ____ Open the box and look at the things.
   ____ Write a date on the box.
   _1_ Get a box.
   ____ Put the box in a place.

4. **YOUR TURN** Work with a partner. Think about your own time capsule. What's in it? Share your ideas.

   > My favorite comic book is in the time capsule. My . . .

DID YOU KNOW...?
The KEO Satellite is a time capsule for space. People around the world write notes online. The notes go in the time capsule.

BE CURIOUS Find out about a group of young scientists. Where are they from? (Workbook p. 75)

Discovery EDUCATION
2.3 YOUNG SCIENTISTS

UNIT 2 REVIEW

Vocabulary

1. Label the personal items.

1. _____
2. _____

3. _____
4. _____

5. _____
6. _____

2. Circle the correct answers.

1. William is **America / American**.
2. The soccer team is from **Brazil / Brazilian**.
3. Martin is **Canada / Canadian**.
4. Is Ms. Kim **Japan / Japanese**?
5. The students are from the **UK / British**.

Grammar

3. Rewrite the sentences. Change the underlined words to possessive adjectives.

1. <u>Jessica's</u> house is red.
   _____

2. <u>The students'</u> English class is at 10:00.
   _____

3. <u>Enrique and my</u> class is on Mondays.
   _____

4. <u>Mr. Wilson's</u> laptop is blue.
   _____

4. Read the answers. Write the questions.

1. A: _____
   B: I'm 13.
2. A: _____
   B: My birthday is October 11.
3. A: _____
   B: My name is Emily.
4. A: _____
   B: I'm from Australia.
5. A: _____
   B: Oliver is my friend.

Useful language

5. Complete the conversation.

| Nice to meet you. | This is | That's | What about you? |

Mike: Hi, I'm Mike.
Lisa: Hi, Mike. I'm Lisa. ¹_____
Mike: You, too. How old are you?
Lisa: I'm 13. ²_____
Mike: I'm 13, too. ³_____ my friend Rob. He's 13, too!
Lisa: Hi, Rob.
Rob: Hi, Lisa.
Lisa: Hey, who's that over there?
Mike: ⁴_____ Mr. Kent. He's my soccer coach.

PROGRESS CHECK: Now I can . . .

☐ identify personal items.
☐ talk about my favorite things.
☐ ask and answer questions about people's background and nationality.
☐ meet, greet, and introduce people.
☐ write a personal profile.
☐ choose things for a time capsule.

CLIL PROJECT
2.4 The Land Down Under, p. 116

3 PEOPLE in my LIFE

Discovery EDUCATION
BE CURIOUS

- Robot Fighters
- What's your phone number? What's your email address?
- My Siberian Family

1. What are the boots like?
2. Who's in the family?
3. How old do you think they are?

UNIT CONTENTS
Vocabulary Family and friends; describing people
Grammar *have*; comparative adjectives; possessive pronouns
Listening A computer game

Vocabulary: Family and friends

My Family and Friends by Sarah Wood

David — Sheila

Richard — Helen   Kate — Paul

Jessie, Me! (Sarah), Tony   Charlie

Jade
The Newton Bears
Jack, Trish, Kyle, and Tami

1. Look at Sarah's scrapbook. Complete the profile about her family with the correct words.

☐ aunt	☐ cousin	☐ grandparents	☐ sister
☐ best friend	☑ father/dad	☐ husband	☐ teammates
☐ brother	☐ grandfather/grandpa	☐ mother/mom	☐ uncle
☐ classmates	☐ grandmother/grandma	☐ parents	☐ wife

Hi. I'm Sarah, and this is my family. Richard is my ¹ _father_, and Helen is my ² _____. They're great ³ _____. Jessie is my ⁴ _____. She's 15. My ⁵ _____ is Tony, and he's 10. My mom's parents are my ⁶ _____. My ⁷ _____'s name is David, and my ⁸ _____'s name is Sheila. My mom's sister is Kate. She's my ⁹ _____, and her ¹⁰ _____, Paul, is my ¹¹ _____. Kate is Paul's ¹² _____. Their son is Charlie. He's my ¹³ _____.

My friends are great, too. Jade is my ¹⁴ _____. She's a lot of fun. Look at my soccer team – the Newton Bears. My ¹⁵ _____ are all girls. Look at the photo of Jack, Trish, Tami, and Kyle. They're my ¹⁶ _____.

 2. Listen, check, and repeat.

3. Complete the diagram with the words for family and friends in Exercise 1.

Male	Male and Female	Female
uncle	teammates	aunt
_____	_____	_____
_____	_____	_____
_____	_____	_____

Speaking: My family tree

4. 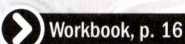 Make a family tree like the one in Sarah's scrapbook. Draw or show pictures of your family members. Then tell your partner about your family.

> This is my mom. Her name is Kendra. She's 43. This is . . .

▶ Workbook, p. 16

Reading A Very Big Family; My Best Friend; Diwali
Conversation On the phone
Writing A description of a person

Do you have A BIG FAMILY?

A Very BIG FAMILY!

Damian is three months old, and he has a BIG family! He has seven sisters and seven brothers! Damian and his family have a big house in Toowoomba, Australia. The house has seven bedrooms! Damian's brother Jesse is 21. He lives away from home, but he's at the house a lot. The other children all live at home with their mom and dad.

Damian's family is very busy. Three of Damian's brothers and sisters have jobs out of the house, and the older kids have work in the house. They are like teammates. They work together and are good friends.

With so many older brothers and sisters in the family, Damian's parents don't have a problem finding a babysitter for baby Damian!

Reading: A web article

1. Look at the title and pictures. What is unusual about Damian's family?

2. Read and listen to the article. Complete the sentences with the correct numbers.

   1. Damian is _____ months old.
   2. He has _____ brothers and sisters.
   3. His brother Jesse is _____ years old.
   4. _____ of his brothers and sisters have jobs.

3. Read the article again. Are the sentences true or false? Write *T* (true), *F* (false), or *NI* (no information). Correct the false sentences.

   1. Damian is an adult. *F. Damian is a baby.*
   2. Damian is American. _____
   3. Jesse has a good job. _____
   4. Damian's family is busy at home. _____
   5. The children aren't very good friends. _____
   6. Damian's parents are out of the house a lot. _____

4. **YOUR TURN** Work with a partner. What is a big family in your opinion? Is your family big, small, or average?

DID YOU KNOW...?
The average number of children in Australian families is 1.9.

Grammar: have

5. Complete the chart.

Use have to talk about possessions, characteristics, and relationships.	
Affirmative	**Negative**
I **have** a brother. Damian _____ a big family. They **have** a big house.	I **don't have** a sister. He **doesn't have** a small family. They _____ **have** a small house.
Yes/No questions	**Short answers**
Do you _____ a brother? **Does** Damian **have** a big family? _____ they **have** a big house?	Yes, I _____. No, I **don't**. Yes, he **does**. No, he _____. Yes, they **do**. No, they **don't**.
Contractions *do not* = _____ *does not* = _____	

> Check your answers: Grammar reference, p. 108

6. Complete the text about Nico's family with the correct forms of *have*.

Hi! I'm Nico, and this is my family. I ¹ *have* a brother and a sister. I'm 11, my brother is 10, and my sister is 8. I ² _____ (not) a baby brother or sister. We ³ _____ very nice parents. We ⁴ _____ a big house, and it ⁵ _____ a yard. We ⁶ _____ a dog, Sparky. My sister wants a cat, but she ⁷ _____ (not) one!

7. Look at the pictures of Jake and Alice. Write yes/no questions.

1. Jake / a book about soccer *Does Jake have a book about soccer?*
2. Alice / inline skates _____
3. Jake and Alice / black shoes _____
4. Jake and Alice / music _____
5. Jake / orange headphones _____

8. Work with a partner. Ask and answer the questions in Exercise 7. For "no" answers, say the correct information.

> Does Jake have a book about soccer?
>
> No, he doesn't. He has a book about basketball.

Jake

Alice

Speaking: Do you have . . . ?

9. YOUR TURN Find someone in your class who can answer "yes" to each question. Ask questions for more information. Complete the chart.

Do you have . . . ?	Name	More information
an older sister	Maria	She's 20.
a baby brother, sister, or cousin		
three (or more) aunts		
a grandparent in your house		

> Do you have an older sister?
>
> Yes, I do.
>
> How old is she?
>
> She's 20.

BE CURIOUS Find out about the Sumii family and the robot event. Who has a robot? (Workbook, p. 76)

Discovery EDUCATION
3.1 ROBOT FIGHTERS

Wow, COOL AVATAR!

Listening: A computer game

1. Do you and your friends play computer games? Which ones?

2. Listen to Carlos and Suzi talk about a computer game. Check (✓) the things in the game.

   ☐ a bike   ☐ a dog   ☐ headphones   ☐ an MP3 player
   ☐ a comic book   ☐ a guitar   ☐ inline skates ☐ a skateboard

3. Listen again. Correct the sentences.
   1. The game is called "My 3D ~~Computer~~." _Home_
   2. The game is in a school. _____
   3. Carlos has 10 points. _____
   4. A bike is 5 points. _____
   5. Suzi's avatar has brown hair. _____

Vocabulary: Describing people

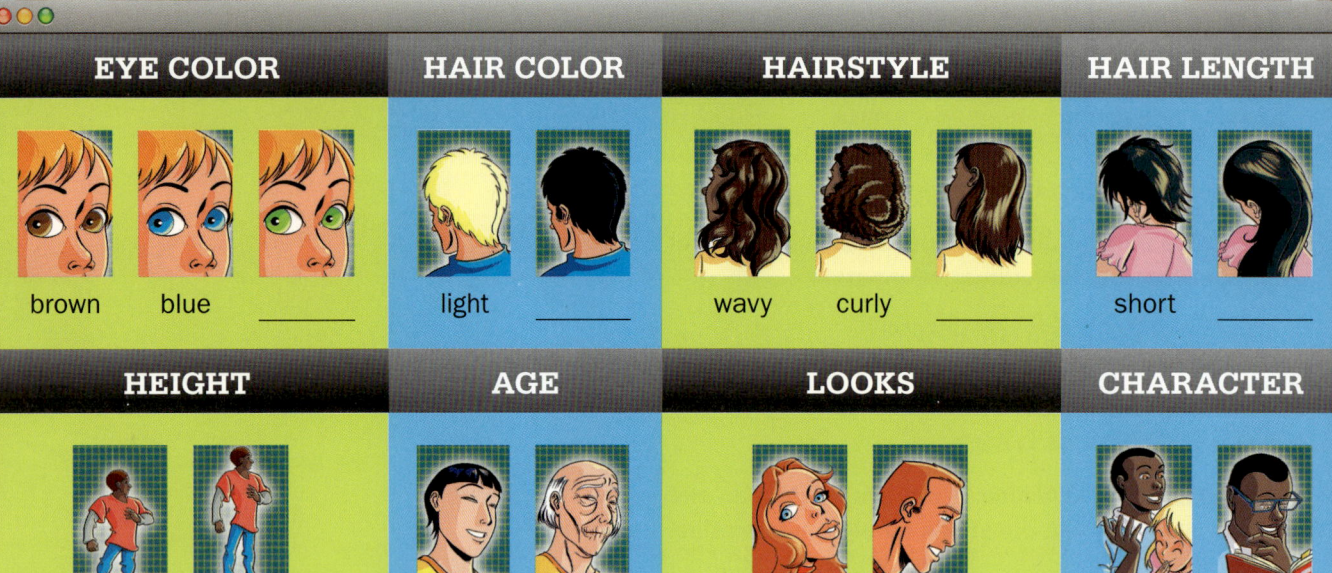

EYE COLOR	HAIR COLOR	HAIRSTYLE	HAIR LENGTH
brown blue ____	light ____	wavy curly ____	short ____

HEIGHT	AGE	LOOKS	CHARACTER
short ____	young ____	pretty ____	funny ____

4. Label the pictures with the correct words. Then listen and check your answers.

dark	long
green	old
handsome	straight
intelligent	tall

5. Create an avatar. Describe it to your partner.

   > My avatar has short hair. Her hair is red. She has brown eyes, and she's intelligent. She's . . .

Grammar: Comparative adjectives

6. Complete the chart.

Use comparative adjectives to show how two things are different from each other.		
1 syllable	dark → dark**er**	My hair is **darker than** his hair.
2 or more syllables	intelligent → **more** intelligent	My avatar is _____ your avatar.
Ending in consonant + -y	wavy → wav**ier**	It's **wavier than** your hair.
Irregular	good → **better** bad → **worse**	Ahmed's avatar is **better than** my avatar. My avatar is _____ his avatar.

> Check your answers: Grammar reference, p. 108

7. Read the sentences. Label the people with the correct names.

1. _____ 2. _____
3. _____

4. _____ 5. _____
6. _____

Dana is shorter than Mari. Mari is taller than Wendy. Dana is taller than Wendy.

Kevin's hair is longer than Pete's hair. Pete's hair is curlier than Mario's hair. Mario's hair is darker than Kevin's hair.

8. Complete the paragraph with comparative adjectives and *than*.

Jim and his brother Brad are very different. Jim is ¹ _younger than_ (young) Brad, but he thinks he is ² _____ (intelligent) his brother. Brad is ³ _____ (funny) Jim. They look different, too. Jim's hair is ⁴ _____ (straight) Brad's hair, and it's also ⁵ _____ (long) Brad's hair. Brad's eyes are ⁶ _____ (dark) Jim's eyes.

> **Say it RIGHT!**
> We stress comparative adjectives but not **than**.
> Listen to the paragraph.
> . . . Jim is **younger than** Brad, but . . .
> Practice with a partner.

9. Write the correct possessive pronouns for the underlined words.

1. Our family is bigger than ~~your family~~. _yours_
2. Her sister is older than his sister.
3. Your eyes are darker than her eyes.
4. My hair is lighter than your hair.
5. Our avatars are better than their avatars.

Possessive pronouns						
Use possessive pronouns to refer to people or things that belong to someone.						
Your avatar is prettier than my avatar. → Your avatar is prettier than **mine**.						
my . . .	your . . .	his . . .	her . . .	your . . .	our . . .	their . . .
mine	**yours**	**his**	**hers**	**yours**	**ours**	**theirs**

Speaking: Family comparisons

10. YOUR TURN Work with a partner. Describe and compare two people in your life. Use the information in the chart. Take turns.

| age | eyes | looks |
| height | hair | character |

My cousin Tom is older than my sister Jill, but Jill is taller than Tom. Tom has brown eyes. Jill's eyes are nicer than his. They're big and green.

> **Get it RIGHT!**
> Don't use **more** before a comparative adjective that ends in **-er**.
> Tom is **older** than Jill.
> NOT: ~~Tom is more older than Jill.~~

> Workbook, pp. 18–19

 **REAL TALK** 3.2 WHAT'S YOUR PHONE NUMBER? WHAT'S YOUR EMAIL ADDRESS?

He's really FUNNY!

Conversation: Talk to you soon.

1. **REAL TALK** Watch or listen to the teenagers. Match the phone numbers with the email addresses.

   1. 937-555-2122 __e__
   2. 845-353-7500 ____
   3. 866-279-9400 ____
   4. 212-337-5000 ____
   5. 662-615-0410 ____
   6. 341-360-7450 ____

   a. racheljane@online.com
   b. steven@schoolemail.com
   c. bertie13@online.com
   d. binny@familyemail.com
   e. emily@familyemail.com
   f. petraiscool@yourmail.com

2. **YOUR TURN** What's *your* phone number? What's *your* email? Tell your partner.

3. Listen to Raul talking to Amy on the phone. Complete the conversation.

USEFUL LANGUAGE: on the phone
Hello? • Hi. It's • Hold on • Can I call you back?

Amy: ¹_____
Raul: ²_____ **Raul**.
Amy: Hi, **Raul**. How are you?
Raul: Good, thanks. Hey, do you have **Ajay's** cell phone number?
Amy: Um, yes. ³_____ a minute. OK. It's **273-270-8951**.
Raul: Thanks. And do you have his email?
Amy: Yes, I do. It's **ajay999@netmail.net**.
Raul: OK, thanks. I want to invite him to the party at my house. He's really funny! Hey, can you come?
Amy: When is it again?
Raul: It's . . . Oh, wait. My mom needs me. ⁴_____
Amy: Sure.
Raul: Good. Talk to you soon.

> **NOTICE IT**
> Use *it's* (not *I'm*) to say who you are on the phone.
> *Hi. **It's** Maria.*
> NOT *Hi. I'm Maria.*

4. Practice the conversation with a partner.

5. **YOUR TURN** Repeat the conversation in Exercise 3, but change the words in purple. Use the information in the chart.

Name	Phone	Email
Maria	899-307-4912	mdulce10@netmail.net
Alex	555-171-8060	alexh@telefonika.com
Vicky	217-222-5176	vwebber@mymail.net
(your own idea)	_____	_____

28 | Unit 3

My Best FRIEND

This week: Jonathan Olsen from Vancouver, Canada

My best friend is my brother David. He's 20 years old. He lives with my mom, my dad, and me in Vancouver. David's very tall. He has dark hair and really green eyes. His hair isn't very long. It's shorter than my hair.

David's a musician, and he's very good. He has five guitars! We both like music, television, and video games. David's really funny, and he's also intelligent. Of course, I'm more intelligent than he is!

Reading to write: Jonathan's best friend

6. Look at the photo. How are Jonathan and his brother similar?

> **Focus on CONTENT**
> A description of a person can include this information:
> - name
> - age
> - relationship (family member or friend)
> - town, country
> - physical characteristics
> - personality
> - job/interests
> - things in common

7. Read the description and answer the questions.
   1. Who is David, and how old is he?
   2. Where is David from?
   3. What is David like? What does he look like?
   4. What are David's interests?

> **Focus on LANGUAGE**
> **Intensifiers**
> Use intensifiers to make adjectives stronger or weaker.
> - very: She's **very** short.
> - really: His hair is **really** fair.
> - not very: The house is **not very** big.

8. Look at the Focus on Language. Find examples of intensifiers in Jonathan's description of his brother.

9. Add the intensifiers to the correct place in each sentence.
   1. Larry's eyes are blue. (really)
      Larry's eyes are really blue.
   2. My sister is intelligent. (very)
   3. Don isn't tall. (not very)
   4. Jenna has curly hair. (really)

Writing: A description of a person

☐ **PLAN**
Choose a friend or family member to describe. Complete their information.

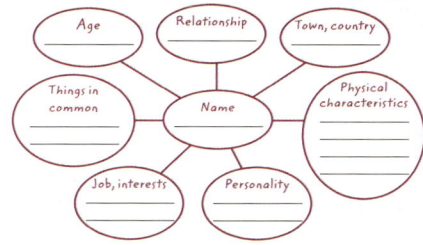

☐ **WRITE**
Now write your description. Use your word web to help you. Write at least 60 words.

☐ **CHECK**
Check your writing. Can you answer "yes" to these questions?

- Do you have information from the Focus on Content box in your description?
- Do you have intensifiers in your description?

Diwali

Diwali is an important Hindu holiday. Raj, 16, is from Mumbai in India. He celebrates Diwali with his family every year.

1 _____

Diwali is a family festival. It's called the "Festival of Lights." It celebrates "good" over "bad" with diyas. Diyas are special lights.

2 _____

Diwali is usually in October or November at the start of the Hindu New Year. The festival has five main days of celebration.

3 _____

People celebrate Diwali in India and in other countries with Hindus, for example, Nepal, Sri Lanka, Malaysia, Singapore, and parts of Europe and the United States.

4 _____

It's important for people and their houses to be clean during Diwali. Clothes are very important during the five days of the festival. The clothes are beautiful and very colorful. Family is also very important. People celebrate with their families at home and eat special meals. It's a wonderful time!

Culture: A family festival

1. **Look at the pictures. What family members do you see?**

2. 🔊 3.08 **Read the magazine interview. Complete the text with the questions. Then listen and check your answers.**

Where is it?	When is it?
What's important during Diwali?	What is Diwali?

3. **Read the text again. Circle the correct answers.**
   1. Diwali is a celebration of **the family / "good" over "bad"**.
   2. Diyas are special **lights / clothes**.
   3. People celebrate Diwali for **two months / five days**.
   4. **People all over the world / Only people in India** celebrate Diwali.
   5. Colorful **clothes / houses** are very important during Diwali.

4. **YOUR TURN** Work with a partner. Do you have a festival similar to Diwali in your country? When is it? How is it special?

   > We have the Chinese New Year. It's in January or February. We . . .

DID YOU KNOW...?
Hindus celebrate a lot of festivals. They have about 40 every year!

BE CURIOUS Find out about a family in Siberia. What family members are in the video? (Workbook, p. 77)

Discovery EDUCATION

3.3 MY SIBERIAN FAMILY

UNIT 3 REVIEW

Vocabulary

1. Look at the pictures. Circle the correct answers.

   1.  He is my **brother / sister / father / mother**.

   2.  They are my **grandmas / grandpas / grandparents / uncles**.

   3.  They are my **cousins / teammates / brothers / sisters**.

   4.  This is my sister's **wife / husband / grandfather / aunt**.

   5. This is my **aunt / uncle / cousins / parents**.

2. Complete the sentences with adjectives to describe people.
   1. Jamie isn't tall. She's _____.
   2. My hair is black. Its color is very _____.
   3. My grandmother isn't young. She's _____.
   4. My hair isn't short. It's very _____.

Grammar

3. Complete the conversation with the correct forms of *have*.

   Mark: ¹_____ you ¹_____ brothers and sisters?

   Julie: Yes. I ²_____ one sister. Her name's Shelly. I ³_____ a brother – it's just my sister and me.

   Mark: Wow. You ⁴_____ a small family.

   Julie: Actually, I ⁵_____ a small family. My family's big. My mom ⁶_____ seven brothers and sisters, and they all ⁷_____ children.

   Mark: ⁸_____ you ⁸_____ a lot of cousins?

   Julie: Yes. I ⁹_____ 25 cousins!

4. Write sentences with comparative adjectives.
   1. Tonya / funny / Terrance
      _____
   2. Wanda's hair / long / Marcia's hair
      _____
   3. Steven / intelligent / Robert
      _____
   4. My avatar / good / your avatar
      _____

Useful language

5. Circle the correct answers.

   Ed: (1) **Hello / Hold on**?

   Lori: Hi, Ed. (2) **I'm / It's** Lori.

   Ed: Oh, hi Lori.

   Lori: Hey, do you have Lydia's cell phone number?

   Ed: Yes, I do. (3) **Hold on / Call back** a minute . . .

   Lori: Sure.

   Ed: OK. Her number is 246-555-2169.

   Lori: Thanks. Do you have her email?

   Ed: I do, but it's on my phone. Can I (4) **hold on / call you back**?

   Lori: Sure. Talk to you soon.

PROGRESS CHECK: Now I can . . .

- ☐ identify my family members and friends.
- ☐ talk about my family.
- ☐ compare people.
- ☐ talk on the phone.
- ☐ write a description of someone.
- ☐ talk about festivals.

4 It's My LIFE!

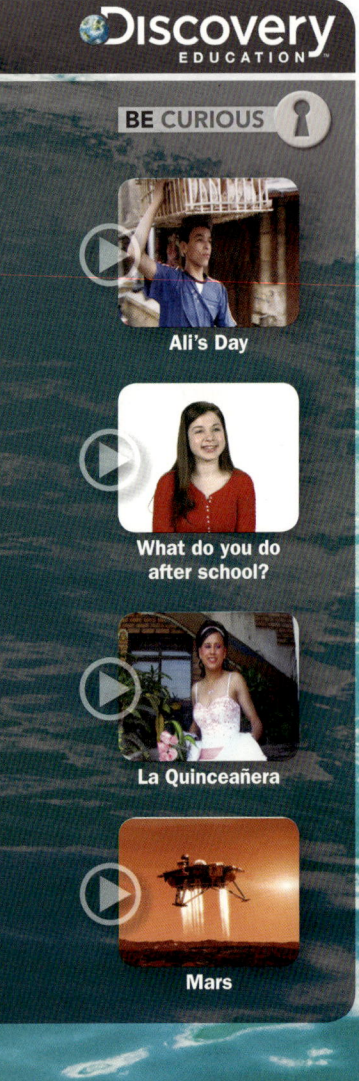

Discovery EDUCATION — BE CURIOUS
- Ali's Day
- What do you do after school?
- La Quinceañera
- Mars

1. Where is he?
2. What activity is this?
3. Do you want to try it?

UNIT CONTENTS
Vocabulary Daily routines; after-school activities
Grammar Simple present statements; simple present questions; adverbs of frequency
Listening Podcast interviews about after-school activities

Vocabulary: Daily routines

1. Match the photos (a–j) with the phrases.

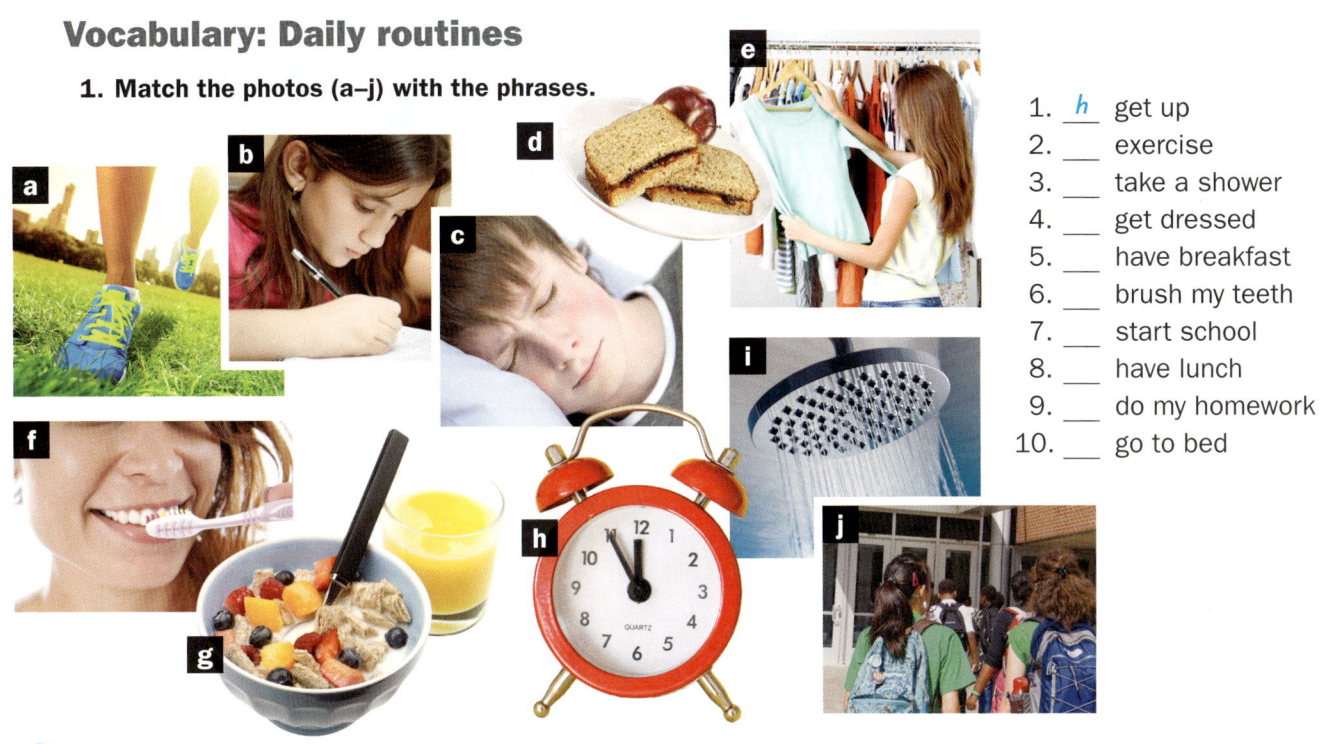

1. _h_ get up
2. ___ exercise
3. ___ take a shower
4. ___ get dressed
5. ___ have breakfast
6. ___ brush my teeth
7. ___ start school
8. ___ have lunch
9. ___ do my homework
10. ___ go to bed

2. Listen, check, and repeat.

3. Complete the article about a typical day in Philip's life. Use the daily routines from Exercise 1.

My name is Philip, and I'm in a stand-up paddle surfing club. We meet very early on Mondays, Wednesdays, and Fridays. On those days, I ^{1} _get up_ at 5:00 in the morning. First I ^{2}_____ in a swimsuit and a T-shirt. Our club meets at 6:00. We ^{3}_____ on the beach and get in the water. By 7:15, I'm back at home and I ^{4}_____. At 7:45 I ^{5}_____, usually some cereal and fresh fruit. I leave for school at 8:05. It isn't far. I ^{6}_____ at 8:30. In the afternoon, we ^{7}_____ at 12:30. Usually, I eat a salad and a sandwich. After school, I like to hang out with friends. Back at home, I ^{8}_____ in the evening after dinner. At night, I always ^{9}_____ before I ^{10}_____

An early morning for Philip Stone, stand-up paddle surfer

4. Listen and check your answers.

Speaking: My routine

5. What is your daily routine? Make a list of things you do. Number them in the correct order.

6. **YOUR TURN** Work with a partner. Talk about your daily routine.

   I get up at 7:00 in the morning. At 7:15, I...

   Workbook, p. 22

NOTICE IT
You can use the verb *eat* or *have* to talk about meals like breakfast, lunch, and dinner. *Have* is more common.
I have breakfast at 7:45. OR
I eat breakfast at 7:45.

Reading Times Around the World; Madison's Blog; It's a New Year!
Conversation Asking for information
Writing A blog post about your routine
CLIL Mars

Unit 4 | 33

She goes to bed LATE!

Times Around the World

- New York, USA 6:00 a.m.
- Rio, Brazil 8:00 a.m.
- Dubai, UAE 3:00 p.m.
- Sydney, Australia 10:00 p.m.

It's 6:00 a.m. in New York City. What time is it in your town?

Barbara It's nighttime here, and I'm in my bedroom. I do my homework at this time during the week. On the weekend, I don't do homework—my family eats dinner in our backyard, and I go to bed late.
19 minutes ago

Renata Wow, is it really night there, Barbara? Amazing! I start classes at school now. It's early in the morning, and I'm tired. My dad teaches at my school, so we go to school together—early!
22 minutes ago

David Hi, Renata and Barbara! I'm at home. I have lunch with my mom and my brother at this time. My brother is two. He doesn't go to school. I love playing with my brother. He's funny! We sleep in the afternoon because it's very hot here.
24 minutes ago

Reading: An online forum

1. Look at the time zone map. When it's 6:00 a.m. in New York, what time is it in your town? What do you do at that time during the week and on the weekend?

2. Read and listen to the posts on the online forum. Where is each person from?

3. Read the posts again. Complete the sentences with *Barbara*, *Renata*, or *David*.

    1. _____ and _____ are at home.
    2. _____ is at school.
    3. _____ does homework at this time.
    4. _____ has lunch at this time.
    5. _____ is tired.

4. **YOUR TURN** Where are you or what do you do at these times? Compare your answers with a partner.

    1. 6:00 a.m. *I'm in bed at 6:00 a.m.*
    2. 8:00 a.m. _____
    3. 3:00 p.m. _____
    4. 10:00 p.m. _____

Grammar: Simple present statements

5. Complete the chart.

Use the simple present to talk about routines, habits, and facts.

Affirmative	Negative
I **start** classes at 8:00 a.m. Renata **starts** classes at 8:00 a.m.	I **don't start** classes at 9:00 a.m. She **doesn't start** classes at 9:00 a.m.
David **goes** to school. Renata and her dad _____ to school together.	David's brother _____ **go** to school. They _____ **go** to different schools.
Contractions do not = _____	does not = _____

Spell it RIGHT!

I/you/we/they	he/she/it
do	does
go	goes
study	stud**ies**
teach	teach**es**

> Check your answers: Grammar reference, p. 109

6. Circle the correct answers.

1. They **speak** / **speaks** English.
2. I **play** / **plays** soccer.
3. We **do** / **does** our homework on the weekend.
4. She **eat** / **eats** at home.
5. They **live** / **lives** in the city.
6. She **study** / **studies** at a university.

7. Make the sentences in Exercise 6 negative.

1. *They don't speak English.*
2. _____
3. _____
4. _____
5. _____
6. _____

8. Complete the blog entry about Jack's family with the simple present forms of the verbs.

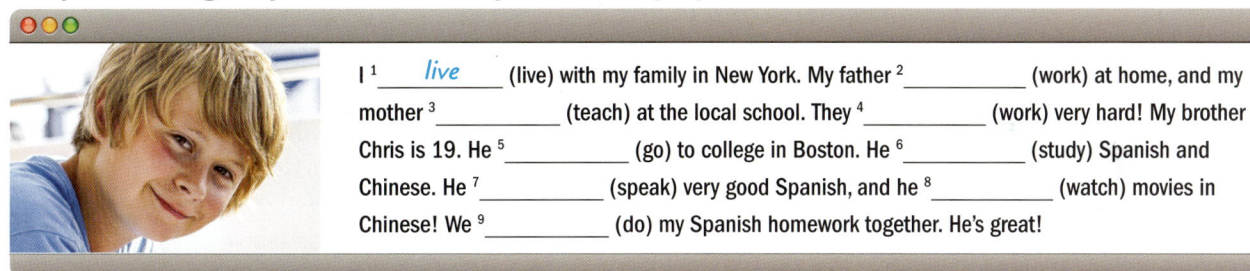

I ¹ *live* (live) with my family in New York. My father ² _____ (work) at home, and my mother ³ _____ (teach) at the local school. They ⁴ _____ (work) very hard! My brother Chris is 19. He ⁵ _____ (go) to college in Boston. He ⁶ _____ (study) Spanish and Chinese. He ⁷ _____ (speak) very good Spanish, and he ⁸ _____ (watch) movies in Chinese! We ⁹ _____ (do) my Spanish homework together. He's great!

Speaking: "Dos" and "Don'ts"

9. Make a list of things you do and don't do during the week, on weekends, and every day.

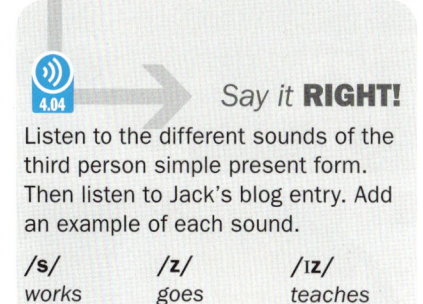

During the week, I . . .	On weekends, I . . .	I . . . every day.
(+)	(+)	(+)
(-)	(-)	(-)

Say it RIGHT!

Listen to the different sounds of the third person simple present form. Then listen to Jack's blog entry. Add an example of each sound.

/s/	/z/	/ɪz/
works	goes	teaches
_____	_____	_____

10. YOUR TURN Work with a partner. Talk about the things you do and don't do.

> During the week, I go to school and . . .

11. Change partners. Share information about your partners from Exercise 10.

> Mia goes to school . . .

BE CURIOUS Find out about Ali's daily routine in Cairo. Is it different from yours? (Workbook, p. 78)

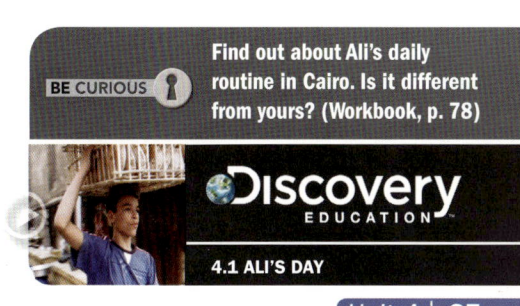

Discovery EDUCATION
4.1 ALI'S DAY

Workbook, pp. 22–23

Busy TEENS

Listening: Podcast interviews

1. What's a podcast? What do you listen to online?
2. Listen to the podcast. What are the interviews about?
3. Listen again. Circle the correct answers.

   1. Sam plays . . .
      a. tennis.   b. chess.   c. tennis and chess.
   2. He doesn't play with . . .
      a. his mom.   b. his brothers.   c. his friends.
   3. Clara has tennis lessons . . .
      a. at school.   b. at home.   c. at the park.
   4. Clara has lessons on . . .
      a. the weekends
      b. Tuesdays and Fridays.
      c. Mondays and Wednesdays.
   5. Clara's dad . . .
      a. is a good player.
      b. isn't a good player.
      c. doesn't play tennis.
   6. Debbie . . .
      a. doesn't play tennis.
      b. plays chess.
      c. doesn't play chess.

Vocabulary: After-school activities

4. Match the words with the pictures. Then listen and check your answers.

   1. _d_ play soccer   5. ___ do karate
   2. ___ play music   6. ___ go swimming
   3. ___ play tennis   7. ___ take dance classes
   4. ___ do drama   8. ___ take art classes

5. Work with a partner. Which activities use a ball? Which ones have special clothing?

36 | Unit 4

Grammar: Simple present questions

6. Complete the chart.

Ask yes/no questions to get short, simple affirmative or negative responses about routines, habits, and facts. Ask Wh- questions to get more specific information.

Yes/No questions	Short answers	Wh- questions
Do you **play** sports?	_____, I **do**. **No,** I **don't**.	Who _____ you **play** chess with? I play with my friends.
_____ Sam **play** sports?	**Yes,** he **does**. **No,** he _____.	Where **does** Sam **play** chess? He plays at school and at home.
Do Clara and her dad _____ sports together?	**Yes,** they **do**. _____, they **don't**.	When **do** they _____? They play on weekends.

> Check your answers: Grammar reference, p. 109

7. Circle *Do* or *Does*. Then answer the questions with your own information.

1. (**Do**) / **Does** you play tennis? _____
2. What **do** / **does** you play? _____
3. **Do** / **Does** your best friend take dance classes? _____
4. Who **do** / **does** you live with? _____
5. Where **do** / **does** your family live? _____
6. **Do** / **Does** your family play music? _____

8. YOUR TURN Add adverbs of frequency to the sentences to make them true for you. Then ask and answer questions with a partner.

1. I brush my teeth after breakfast.
2. I get up early on weekends.
3. I play sports after school.
4. I hang out with my friends after school.
5. I watch TV in bed.
6. I am late for school.

> Do you brush your teeth after breakfast?
>> Yes, I always brush my teeth after breakfast.

Adverbs of frequency

always — usually — often — sometimes — never

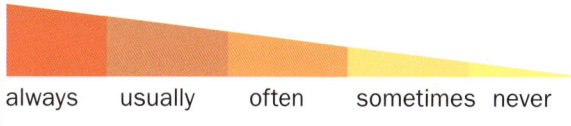

How **often** do you play sports?
I **never** play sports.
Where do you play tennis?
We **often** play at the club.
Sometimes, we play at the park.

Speaking: Yes or no?

9. YOUR TURN Work with a partner. Ask *yes/no* questions about these topics. Ask *Wh-* questions for more information.

after-school activities   morning routines   clubs and sports

> Do you play sports after school?
>> Yes, I do.
> What do you play?
>> I often play soccer. Sometimes, I play tennis.

10. Change partners. Share information about your partners from Exercise 9.

> Daniel often plays soccer after school. Sometimes, he . . .

Get it RIGHT!

Adverbs of frequency usually come after the verb *be*, but before other verbs.
I'm **never** late. I **never** get to class late. NOT: ~~I get **never** to class late.~~
Usually and **sometimes** may come before the subject.
I **usually** get up early. **Usually**, I get up early.

> Workbook, pp. 24–25

REAL TALK 4.2 WHAT DO YOU DO AFTER SCHOOL?

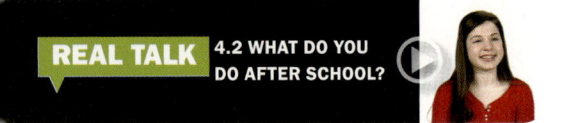

At the GYM

Conversation: I'd like some information, please.

1. **REAL TALK** Watch or listen to the teenagers. What do they do after school? Check (✓) the activities.

   - ☐ dance
   - ☐ do homework
   - ☐ do karate
   - ☐ eat dinner
   - ☐ go to the gym
   - ☐ play basketball
   - ☐ play soccer
   - ☐ play video games
   - ☐ practice violin
   - ☐ read
   - ☐ ride a bike
   - ☐ watch television

2. **YOUR TURN** What do *you* do after school? Tell your partner.

3. Listen to Bob on the phone with a receptionist. Complete the conversation.

USEFUL LANGUAGE: Asking for Information

How much | What time | Do you have | What days

Gemma: Hello, Pompano Beach Gym. This is Gemma. How can I help you?

Bob: Hi, Gemma. I'd like some information, please. ¹_____ **karate classes** at the gym?

Gemma: Yes, we do.

Bob: Great! ²_____ are the classes?

Gemma: They're on **Wednesdays**.

Bob: OK. ³_____ are the classes?

Gemma: They're from **5:30 to 6:45**.

Bob: That's good. And ⁴_____ are they?

Gemma: The price is **$5** a class.

Bob: Perfect, thanks!

Gemma: You're welcome. Have a nice day!

Bob: Thanks, you too. Bye!

4. Practice the conversation with a partner.

5. **YOUR TURN** Repeat the conversation in Exercise 3, but change the words in purple. Use the information in the schedule.

Pompano Beach Gym: Schedule of Classes

Class Type	Day	Time	Price per class
Gymnastics	M W	5:30–6:30pm	$5
Swimming	T Th	7:00–8:00pm	$7
Karate	W	5:30–6:45pm	$5
Kickboxing	Th	5:45–6:45pm	$6
Dance	M F	6:45–7:45pm	$5

MADISON FINLAY
CHAMPION SWIMMER

ASK ME A QUESTION.

Hi Madison,
My question is: What is your routine before the world championships?
Chloe
P.S. Good luck!

Hi Chloe,
I always get up at 6:45, and I have a big breakfast. I start school at 8:08 (really!) and finish at 2:15. I usually have lunch at the pool with the other swimmers. For four hours in the afternoon, I swim in the pool and exercise at the gym. I get home at around 7:30. After dinner, I do my homework. Sometimes I watch TV or chat online with my friends before bed. I go to bed at 10:00 or 10:30. On weekends, I go to the pool for six hours, but on Saturday evening, I always hang out with my friends.

Reading to write: Madison's blog

6. Look at the the photo. Do you think Madison's daily routine is easy or difficult? Read her blog to check.

● Focus on CONTENT
When you write about daily routines, put information in chronological order, from morning to night. Write about your weekdays first. Put the weekend at the end.

7. Read Madison's blog again. What does she do at these times?

   1. 6:45 a.m.   3. 2:15 p.m.   5. 10:30 p.m.
   2. 8:08 a.m.   4. 7:30 p.m.

● Focus on LANGUAGE
Connectors: *and, but, or*
- Use *and* to show ideas in order: *I have breakfast **and** brush my teeth.*
- Use *but* to contrast two ideas: *I exercise every day, **but** I don't go to the gym.*
- Use *or* to show two possibilities: *We talk on the phone **or** chat online after school.*

8. Find the uses of *and*, *but*, and *or* in Madison's blog.

9. Complete the sentences with the correct connectors.

   1. I get up ___*and*___ take a shower.
   2. I usually eat breakfast at 8:00 _____ 8:30.
   3. I get up at 6:30 during the week, _____ on weekends, I get up at 8:00.
   4. I finish school at 3:00 _____ start basketball practice at 3:15.

Writing: Your routine

○ **PLAN**
Make a list of things you usually do during the week and on the weekend. Then number them in the order you do them.

During the week	On weekends

○ **WRITE**
Now write your blog post. Use your notes from Step 1 and Madison's blog to help you. Write 80–100 words.

○ **CHECK**
Check your writing. Can you answer "yes" to these questions?

- Is the information in chronological order?
- Do you have examples of *and*, *but*, and *or*?

Workbook, pp. 26–27

It's a New Year!

10, 9, 8, 7, 6, 5, 4, 3, 2, 1... Happy New Year!

_____

In many places, New Year's Eve is December 31, and New Year's Day is January 1. The New Year starts at midnight. Because of different time zones, it's not midnight at the same time everywhere. People in Kiritimati, an island in the Pacific Ocean, are the first people to "say hello" to the New Year. People on Howard Island, between Australia and Hawaii, are the last.

_____

Many countries have similar New Year's Eve celebrations. They dance, sing, and make music. They watch fireworks. In New York City, a big ball drops at midnight. Thousands of people come and watch. They count down the last 10 seconds before midnight, and then the ball drops. People around the world watch this on TV.

_____

Not all celebrations are the same. For example, in Spain and Ecuador, people eat 12 grapes, one for each month, before midnight. They make a wish for each grape. In Australia, people have parties at night on New Year's Eve, and they have picnics on the beach on New Year's Day. In France and Greece, people give each other presents for the New Year.

Culture: The New Year

1. **Look at the title and the photos. Why do you think people celebrate the New Year?**

2. **Read the article. Complete the text with the headings. Then listen and check your answers.**

   Unusual Ways to Celebrate

   Same Celebration, Different Times

   Common Ways to Celebrate

3. **Read the article again. Match the activities with the places.**

   1. ___ Kiritimati   a. People eat grapes.
   2. ___ Howard Island   b. People give gifts.
   3. ___ New York City   c. People celebrate the New Year last.
   4. ___ Ecuador   d. People celebrate at the beach.
   5. ___ Australia   e. People celebrate the New Year first.
   6. ___ France   f. People watch a ball drop.

4. **YOUR TURN** Work with a partner. Do you celebrate the New Year? What do you usually do?

   > We always have a party on December 31. We usually eat . . .

DID YOU KNOW...?

Some cultures celebrate the New Year on a different day. For example, the Chinese New Year is in mid-January or in February.

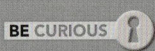

BE CURIOUS Find out about Priscilla's 15th birthday. What does she wear? (Workbook, p. 79)

Discovery EDUCATION

4.3 LA QUINCEAÑERA

40 | Unit 4

UNIT 4 REVIEW

Vocabulary

1. Look at the pictures. Write sentences about David's morning routine.

1. *He gets up.*
2. _____
3. _____
4. _____
5. _____

Grammar

2. Complete the sentences with the simple present forms of the verbs.

1. I ___*like*___ (like) basketball.
2. My sister never _____ (play) tennis.
3. We usually _____ (eat) lunch at home.
4. My brother _____ (go) to a university.
5. He _____ (study) English.
6. We _____ (not go) to bed early on weekends.

3. Write yes/no and Wh- questions with the information below.

1. Cindy and Phil / take art classes
   (yes/no) _____
   (where) _____
2. Nicole / play the piano
   (yes/no) _____
   (why) _____
3. Michael / go swimming
   (yes/no) _____
   (how often) _____
4. you and Scott / play soccer
   (yes/no) _____
   (when) _____

Useful language

4. Complete the conversation.

How much	What time	Do you have	What days

A: Hello. How can I help you?
B: Hi. ¹_____ judo classes here?
A: Yes, we do. We have beginner and intermediate classes.
B: ²_____ are the beginner classes?
A: They meet on Mondays and Wednesdays.
B: ³_____ do the classes start?
A: They start at 4:30.
B: ⁴_____ are they?
A: Let's see. Judo classes are $20 a month.
B: Great. Thanks!

PROGRESS CHECK: Now I can . . .

- ☐ talk about my daily routine.
- ☐ talk about things I do and don't do.
- ☐ ask and answer questions about routines and activities.
- ☐ ask questions for more information.
- ☐ write a blog about my routine.
- ☐ discuss a special occasion.

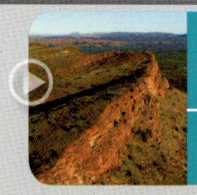

CLIL PROJECT
4.4 Mars, p. 117

UNITS 3–4 REVIEW, Workbook, pp. 28–29

5 School DAYS

Discovery EDUCATION

BE CURIOUS

- Kung Fu School
- Can you use your cell phone at school?
- Tobilay's School Day

1. What do you see in the photo?

2. Where are the students?

3. Do you do activities like this?

UNIT CONTENTS

Vocabulary Places at school; school subjects
Grammar can for ability; object pronouns; verb + -ing form (gerund) for opinions
Listening A student's experience at a performing arts school

Vocabulary: Places at school

1. Where are the people and things? Label the pictures with the correct words.

a cafeteria	a gym	a science lab	an auditorium
a classroom	a library	an art room	✓ the main office
a computer lab	a playground		

1. _the main office_
2. _____
3. _____
4. _____
5. _____
6. _____
7. _____
8. _____
9. _____
10. _____

🔊 **2.** Listen, check, and repeat.
5.01

3. Where do these things happen? Write the places from Exercise 1.

1. We have lunch in this place.
   a cafeteria
2. We have school concerts here. _____
3. We play outside here. _____
4. We do indoor sports here. _____
5. We work on computers here. _____
6. We do experiments in this place. _____
7. We learn about many subjects here. _____
8. We get books in this place. _____
9. We go to this place to ask questions. _____
10. We make pictures in this place. _____

Speaking: Your school

4. **YOUR TURN** Work with a partner. Which places from Exercise 1 are in your school? What do you do there? What's your favorite place? Why?

> We don't have an auditorium. We have a cafeteria. We buy lunch or bring our own and eat it in the cafeteria. We have . . .

5. Join another pair. Tell them about your partner's favorite place.

> Cara's favorite place is the science lab. She thinks the experiments are fun.

▶ Workbook, p. 30

Reading Kung Fu School; Using the Computer Lab; A Do-It-Yourself School
Conversation Asking for and giving permission
Writing An email asking for permission

Unit 5 | 43

I can do KUNG FU!

Kung Fu School

Kung fu is a martial art, and it's also a great Chinese tradition. Many Chinese children go to special schools and study kung fu every day! Some schools have 10,000 students! Some students live at kung fu schools away from their homes. After the students finish their studies, they can often get good jobs.

Li Zheng is a 13-year-old kung fu student from Shanghai. She lives at a kung fu school in Beijing and only sees her family during vacations. She practices kung fu every day with hundreds of other students. She wants to be a police officer in the future. Every morning and evening, Li practices her kung fu moves for hours. What can she do? She can do a lot of moves, like the frog, the dragon, and the snake! She can't break a brick with her hands yet, but her teacher can!

DID YOU KNOW...?
Some martial arts are over 2,000 years old!

Reading: An article about kung fu

1. Look at the title and photos. Do you know anyone who does kung fu? Do you know any other kung fu moves?

2. Read and listen to the article. Where does Li Zheng go to school?

3. Read the article again. Correct the sentences.
   1. Kung fu is a Japanese tradition. _____
   2. Li's kung fu school is small. _____
   3. Li lives with her family. _____
   4. Li wants to be a kung fu teacher. _____
   5. Li practices her moves one time every day.
   _____

4. **YOUR TURN** Work with a partner. What do you think of Li's school?

   I like Li's school. Kung fu is fun.

   I don't like it. She practices with hundreds of students. It's difficult to learn in big classes.

44 | Unit 5

Grammar: *can* for ability

5. Complete the chart.

Use *can* to express what someone or something is able or not able to do.	
Affirmative	**Negative**
I **can do** kung fu. Li's teacher _____ **break** a brick.	I **can't do** karate. Li _____ a brick.
Questions	**Answers**
Can he **break** a brick? What _____ she **do**?	Yes, he _____. / No, he **can't**. She **can do** a lot of moves.
Contraction cannot = _____	

> Check your answers: Grammar reference, p. 110

6. Rewrite each sentence to make it negative. Then write an affirmative sentence with the extra information.

1. You can play the violin. (the guitar) *You can't play the violin. You can play the guitar.*
2. I can swim 100 meters. (50 meters) _____
3. Lenny and Olga can speak Spanish. (English) _____
4. We can play tennis. (soccer) _____
5. My phone can play music. (my laptop) _____

7. Look at the chart. Write questions (Q) and answers (A).

	Do kung fu	Dance	Sing	Play basketball
Sonia	✓	✓	✓	
Jim		✓	✓	

1. Sonia / dance
   Q: *Can Sonia dance?*
   A: *Yes, she can.*

2. Jim / do kung fu
   Q: _____
   A: _____

3. Sonia and Jim / sing
   Q: _____
   A: _____

4. Sonia and Jim / play basketball
   Q: _____
   A: _____

Say it RIGHT!
Listen to the different vowel sounds in **can** and **can't**.
Can you sing? Yes, I **can**.
/ə/   /æ/
No, I **can't**, but I **can** dance!
    /æ/   /æ/
Listen and repeat the questions and answers in Exercise 7. Then practice with a partner.

Get it RIGHT!
Use **well**, not **good**, to modify verbs, such as those for abilities.
I can sing very **well**.
NOT: ~~I can sing very good~~.

Speaking: What can you do?

8. YOUR TURN Work with a partner. What activities can your partner do?

> Can you dance?
>
> Yes, I can. I can dance very well.

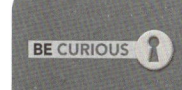

BE CURIOUS: Find out about a kung fu school in China. How many boys are at the school? (Workbook p. 80)

Discovery EDUCATION
5.1 KUNG FU SCHOOL

STUDYING and PERFORMING

Listening: It's a really good school!

1. Look at the photo of Tom at school. What kind of school do you think he goes to?

2. Listen to Tom talk about his school. Check your answer to Exercise 1. What classes does he have?

3. Listen again. Are the sentences true or false? Write *T* (true), *F* (false), or *NI* (no information).

   1. Tom does well in all of his classes. _____
   2. He has seven classes a day. _____
   3. He never has homework on the weekends. _____
   4. He sometimes goes to music concerts. _____
   5. Tom wants to be a singer. _____
   6. Tom's parents come to his performances. _____

Vocabulary: School subjects

4. Match the words with the pictures. Then listen and check your answers.

   1. _e_ art
   2. ____ civics
   3. ____ English
   4. ____ geography
   5. ____ history
   6. ____ ICT
   7. ____ math
   8. ____ PE
   9. ____ science
   10. ____ Spanish

   NOTICE IT
   ICT = information communication technology
   PE = physical education

5. **YOUR TURN** Work with a partner. What school subjects do you have? What are your favorite subjects? What subjects can you do well?

Grammar: Object pronouns; verb + -ing form (gerund) for opinions

6. Complete the chart.

Subject pronoun	Object pronoun
I	me
he	him
she	her
it	_____
you	you
we	_____
they	them

Use object pronouns to replace nouns that follow verbs. They receive the action of the verb.

I love my <u>dance class</u>. → I love **it**.
Tom takes <u>art classes</u> in the morning. → He takes **them** in the morning.
They give <u>homework</u> to <u>my classmates and me</u>. → They give _____ to **us**.

Use -ing forms (gerunds) after certain verbs to express opinions. Use the object pronoun it *to replace these -ing forms and phrases.*

😀 love   🙂 like   😐 don't mind   🙁 don't like   😖 hate

Tom _____ <u>dancing</u>. → He loves **it**.
I **don't mind** _____ <u>homework</u>. → I don't mind _____.
Do you **like** <u>playing the guitar</u>? → Do you like **it**?

> Check your answers: Grammar reference, p. 110

7. Replace the underlined nouns with subject or object pronouns.

My favorite subject is geography. I really like ¹<u>geography</u> (*it*). I usually sit with Eva. She's my best friend. The teacher often asks ²<u>Eva</u> to read in class. Then ³<u>Eva and I</u> have Spanish with Mr. Gomez. Eva really likes ⁴<u>Mr. Gomez</u>, and she loves Spanish, too. ⁵<u>Eva</u> can speak ⁶<u>Spanish</u> really well! Sometimes, she helps me with ⁷<u>Spanish</u>. In PE, ⁸<u>Eva and I</u> sometimes play tennis with our friends, John and Thomas. ⁹<u>John and Thomas</u> don't like playing tennis with ¹⁰<u>Eva and me</u>, but we like playing with ¹¹<u>John and Thomas</u> because we usually win! We're really good at ¹²<u>playing tennis</u>!

8. Write sentences to express opinions. Add your own opinions with the object pronoun.

1. Rick / play soccer 🙁
   Rick doesn't like playing soccer.   *I like it.*

2. they / studying math 😐
   _____   _____

3. Ahmed / speak English 😀
   _____   _____

4. Pam and Gracie / do homework 😖
   _____   _____

5. Tonya / run 🙂
   _____   _____

Speaking: Do you like it?

9. YOUR TURN Ask and answer the questions with a partner.

1. Do you like vacations?
2. Do you like history?
3. Do you like making art?
4. Do you like doing experiments?
5. Do you like working on computers?
6. Do you like studying geography?

> Do you like vacations?
> Yes, I love them!

REAL TALK 5.2 CAN YOU USE YOUR CELL PHONE AT SCHOOL?

ASKING for It!

Conversation: What do you want?

1. **REAL TALK** Watch or listen to the teenagers. How many of them can't use their phones at school?

2. **YOUR TURN** Can *you* use *your* cell phone at school? Tell your partner.

3. Listen to Julia asking her teacher for permission to do something. Complete the conversation.

> **USEFUL LANGUAGE: Asking for and giving permission**
> Can I   May I   I'm sorry, but   Sure, no problem.

Julia: Excuse me. Ms. Martin?
Ms. Martin: Yes, Julia. What do you want?
Julia: ¹_____ call my mom on my cell phone?
Ms. Martin: ²_____ no cell phones in class.
Julia: I know, Ms. Martin. But **my little brother is sick, and I have his medicine!**
Ms. Martin: I see.
Julia: ³_____ call her from the main office?
Ms. Martin: ⁴_____
Julia: Thanks, Ms. Martin.

4. Practice the conversation with a partner.

5. **YOUR TURN** Repeat the conversation in Exercise 3, but change the words in purple. Use the information in the chart.

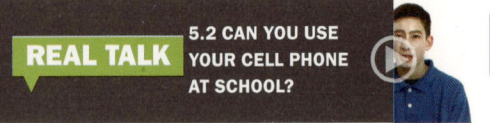

Request 1	Reason why not	Reason why it's important	Request 2
go to my brother's class	you can't leave the classroom	I have his homework in my bag	give it to him at lunchtime
go to the gym	it's time for math	my tennis shoes are there	go after math
_____ (your own idea)	_____	_____	_____

48 | Unit 5

To: lee@jjmiddleschool.cup/org
From: k.jones@net.cup/org
Subject: Using the computer lab

Dear Mr. Lee,

I'm Kylie Jones, and I'm in your computer class. My friends and I want to make a website for our soccer team. We need computers to do it. We want to work together at the same time, but we don't have laptops. May we use the computer lab after school on Wednesdays at 4:00? We also need some help with the website. Can you help us with it?

Please let me know. Thank you for thinking about this.

Sincerely,
Kylie

Reading to write: Kylie's email request

6. Look at the photo. What problem do the students have?

> *Focus on* **CONTENT**
> In an email asking for permission:
> 1. Introduce yourself.
> 2. State the problem.
> 3. Ask for permission to do something.
> 4. Say thank you.

7. Read the email again. What's Kylie's problem? What does she ask for permission to do?

> *Focus on* **LANGUAGE**
> **A formal email**
> In a formal email, include:
> - a short subject line with the main idea: *Needing a laptop, Help with homework*
> - a greeting: *Dear Mrs. Campbell, Hi Mr. Sanchez,*
> - a closing: *Sincerely, Best regards*

8. What is Kylie's subject line? What greeting and closing does she use?

9. Choose the correct expressions for a formal email to a teacher about a test.

1. Subject line:
   a. Study help   b. Where are you?   c. Come to my house

2. Greeting:
   a. Hey there,   b. Hello Ms. Cooper,   c. Hi, teacher!

3. Closing:
   a. Bye-bye!   b. Your friend,   c. Best regards,

Writing: An email request

PLAN
Think of a problem and something to ask permission for. Write notes in the chart.

Problem	Request

WRITE
Now write an email to someone at your school about your problem and request. Use your chart to help you. Write at least 60 words.

CHECK
Check your writing. Can you answer "yes" to these questions?

- Is information from the Focus on Content box in your email?
- Do you have an appropriate subject line, greeting, and closing?

Imagine a school with only one rule and no tests. This school is Brightworks! Brightworks is in San Francisco, California. The students are 5 to 14 years old, and they make things together. The school's one rule is: "Don't hurt yourself or anyone else."

A DO-IT-YOURSELF School

Students have a topic each year. They learn about the topic in three steps.

❶ Exploration
Students explore the topic. Let's say the topic is "the earth." Students learn about the earth through history, art, math, science, and other subjects. They can study maps of land and water. They can interview a weather person. They can do experiments with the earth.

❷ Expression
Students think of a project. They ask for tools and help from Brightworks teachers. For the topic "the earth," students can make a greenhouse for plants, or they can write a play about the earth.

❸ Exposition
Students share their projects with their families and the community. They can give them a tour of their greenhouse, or they can perform their play for them. Their projects are also online.

Culture: An unusual school

1. Look at the photos. What do you see?

2. Read and listen to the article. Match the steps (1–3) with the photos (a–c).

   1. Exploration _____   2. Expression _____   3. Exposition _____

3. Read the article again. Answer the questions.

   1. Where is Brightworks? _____

   2. How old are the students? _____

   3. How do they learn about the year's topic? _____

   4. Who do they ask for help? _____

   5. Who do they show their projects to? _____

4. **YOUR TURN** Work with a partner. What do you think of Brightworks? What are some interesting or unusual things about your school?

   > I think Brightworks is . . .

   > In our school, we have an unusual cafeteria. The food is really good, and the students make it!

DID YOU KNOW . . . ?
DIY is short for *do it yourself*. DIY projects are popular with teens and adults in the United States.

BE CURIOUS Find out about Tobilay's school day. What does she do at school? (Workbook p. 81)

Discovery EDUCATION
5.3 TOBILAY'S SCHOOL DAY

50 | Unit 5

UNIT 5 REVIEW

Vocabulary

1. Where in a school can you find these things? Write the places.

   1. _____
   2. _____
   3. _____
   4. _____
   5. _____
   6. _____

2. Put the letters in order to make school subjects.

   1. icsnece _____
   2. sccvii _____
   3. shnelig _____
   4. atmh _____
   5. ortihsy _____
   6. hagegorpy _____
   7. TIC _____
   8. aihpsns _____

Grammar

3. Write sentences and questions with the correct form of *can*.

   1. he / ride a bike (?) _____
   2. Maria / dance (✓) _____
   3. we / play tennis / at all (✗) _____
   4. you / swim (?) _____
   5. they / do kung fu (✓) _____

4. Complete the text with the correct object pronouns.

   Zara is my best friend. I like [1]_____, and she likes [2]_____! We're in the same class. Our teacher is Mr. Stevens. I don't like [3]_____ because he gives [4]_____ a lot of homework. Zara loves art, but I hate [5]_____. Our friends like playing soccer, and we like [6]_____, too! We often play after school with [7]_____.

5. Complete the sentences with the –*ing* form of the correct verbs.

   | do | eat | play | read | watch |

   1. I don't mind _____ my homework.
   2. I love _____ games on my computer.
   3. I hate _____ in the cafeteria.
   4. I like _____ comic books.
   5. I don't like _____ TV.

Useful language

6. Circle the correct answers.

   Ben: Hey, Jack. (1) **Can I / Do I** use your laptop?
   Jack: (2) **I'm sorry / Sure, no problem**. Here.
   Ben: OK. Thanks!
   Jack: Oh, and (3) **I may / may I** use your game console?
   Ben: (4) **I'm sorry, but / Sure, no problem**. I want to use it now.

PROGRESS CHECK: Now I can . . .

- ☐ identify places at my school.
- ☐ talk about my abilities.
- ☐ express opinions about school subjects and activities.
- ☐ ask for and give permission.
- ☐ write an email asking for permission to do something.
- ☐ discuss interesting or unusual things about schools.

Uncover Your Knowledge

UNITS 1–5 Review Game

TEAM 1 — START

1. Introduce yourself. Say your name, nationality, and the languages you speak.
2. Look around the classroom. Identify five different objects and their colors.
3. Say seven subject pronouns in 30 seconds.
4. What are three school subjects you like? What are two school subjects you don't like?
5. Tell your teammate the names of four other people in the class. Use *This is* or *That's* correctly.
6. Give examples of two personal items related to each category: music, technology, and sports.
7. Ask your teammate three questions about his or her family. Your teammate answers the questions.
8. What are five instructions teachers usually give? Say them in one minute.
9. You want to sign up for a class at the gym. Call your teammate for information. Ask and answer three different questions.
10. Ask your teammate if he or she likes five different school subjects. Your teammate answers with the object pronoun.
11. Ask your teammate about his or her name, nationality, age, and birthday.

INSTRUCTIONS:

- Make teams and choose game pieces.
- Put your game pieces on your team's START.
- Flip a coin to see who goes first.
- Read the first challenge. Can you do it correctly?

　　Yes → Continue to the next challenge.

　　No → Lose your turn.

The first team to do all of the challenges wins!

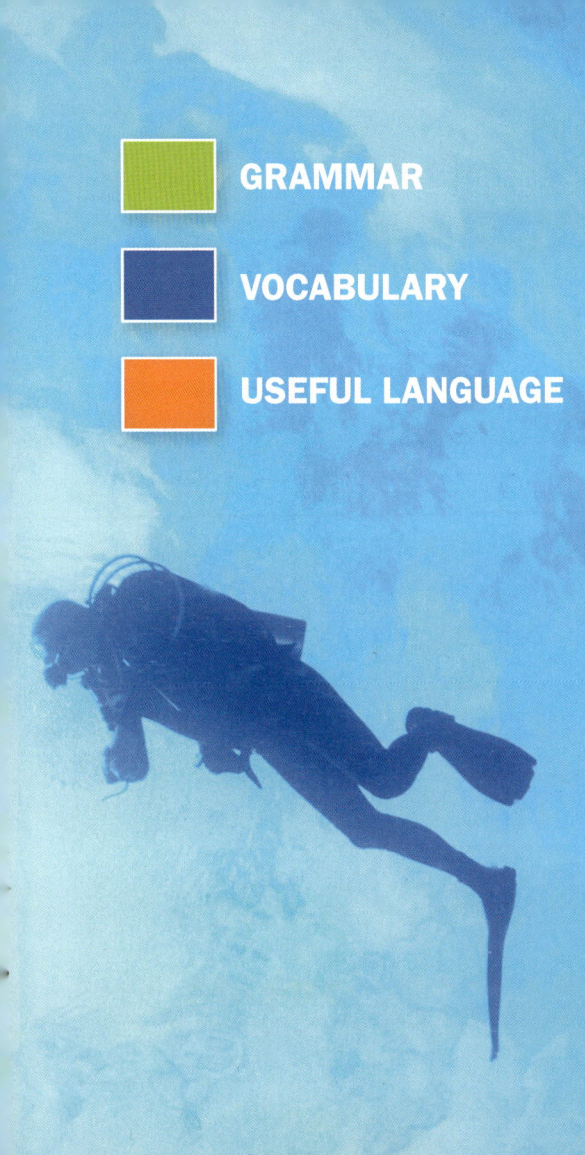

- GRAMMAR
- VOCABULARY
- USEFUL LANGUAGE

TEAM 2
START

1. Spell your first name and last name.
2. Name 10 words for family members in 30 seconds.
3. What are four rules in your classroom? Give two affirmative rules and two negative ones.
4. What do you do after school on weekdays? Give four examples.
5. Ask to use your teammate's laptop or phone. Say why. Your teammate responds.
6. What are four things you do in the morning?
7. Look around the room. Make sentences about things you see using *my*, *their*, *our*, and *'s*.
8. Name three places in your school. Explain what happens in these places in one minute.
9. Compare yourself with your best friend. Say two ways you are the same and two ways you are different.
10. Does your teammate do any after-school activities? Ask about four different activities.
11. Call your teammate. Ask for someone's phone number and email address. Your teammate answers.
12. Describe your teammate. Say something about his or her eye color, hair color, hairstyle, hair length, height, age, and character.
13. In one minute, say three things you always do and three things you never do on the weekends.
14. What talents or abilities do you have? Give three examples.

Units 1–5 Review | 53

Simple present of be and subject pronouns, p. 5

Use the simple present of be to identify people and give locations and dates.

Affirmative			Negative		
I	am	a photographer.	I	am not	a musician.
He/She/It	is	12 years old.	He/She/It	is not	13 years old.
You/We/They	are	on the football field.	You/We/They	are not	in the gym.
Yes/No questions			**Short answers**					
Am	I	in your class?	Yes,	you	are.	No,	you	are not.
Are	you	a photographer?		I	am.		I	am not.
Is	he/she/it	12 years old?		he/she/it	is.		he/she/it	is not.
Are	we/they	on the football field?		we/they	are.		we/they	are not.

You can use subject pronouns instead of names to refer to people or things. You can use contractions to combine subject pronouns with the simple present be.

Subject pronouns	Affirmative contractions	Negative contractions
I	I am = I'm	I am not = I'm not
you	you are = you're	you are not = you're not / you aren't
he	he is = he's	he is not = he's not / he isn't
she	she is = she's	she is not = she's not / she isn't
it	it is = it's	it is not = it's not / it isn't
we	we are = we're	we are not = we're not / we aren't
they	they are = they're	they are not = they're not / they aren't

1. Complete the conversations with the correct subject pronouns and the simple present of be. Use contractions when possible.

   1. **A:** Is Tonya 18 years old? **B:** No, _____.
   2. Wendy and Max _____ students. _____ in my class.
   3. **A:** Are you on a football team? **B:** Yes, _____.
   4. **A:** Am I in Room C? **B:** No, _____. _____ in Room D.

Imperatives, p. 7

Use imperatives to give commands or instructions.

Affirmative			Negative		
Close	the door.			close	the door.
Turn	to page 7.		Don't	turn	to page 8.
Meet	on the soccer field.			meet	in the gym.
Contraction	do not = **don't**				

2. Put the words in the correct order to make sentences.

   1. the / teacher / listen / to _____
   2. in / talk / library / don't / the _____
   3. gym, please / in / meet / the _____
   4. page / your book / 23 / open / to _____

Possessives, p. 15

Use a possessive adjective or a name/noun + 's to show possession. For plural subjects, add s'.

Subject pronouns	Possessive adjectives	
I	my	**My** laptop is new.
you	your	**Your** class is in Room B.
he	his	**His** name is Jerry.
she	her	**Her** boat is pink.
it	its	**Its** name is *Pink Lady*.
we	our	**Our** parents are from Japan.
they	their	**Their** skateboards are blue.

Possessive 's or s'

Jessica's boat is pink. The **boat's** name is *Pink Lady*.
Carlos's favorite color is blue.
The **boats'** names are *Blue Whale* and *Pink Lady*.
Our **parents'** car is new.

1. Write sentences two ways. Use possessive 's and possessive adjectives.

1. Lydia / sneakers are blue

   Lydia's sneakers are blue.   Her sneakers are blue.

2. The dog / ball is red

   _____   _____

3. The teachers / names are Mr. Lark and Mrs. Moore

   _____   _____

4. Andrew / parents are from Brazil

   _____   _____

Question words, p. 17

Use Wh- questions to ask about specific information.

Question word	be	Subject	Answer
Where	are	you from?	Canada.
What	is	your favorite thing?	My guitar.
Who	are	your classmates?	Felipe and Rachel.
When	is	your birthday?	September 21.

Question word + adjective or noun	be	Subject	Answer
How old	are	you?	12.
What time	is	it?	It's 3:00.
Contractions	Where is = **Where's** Who is = **Who's**	What is = **What's** When is = **When's**	

2. Circle the correct question words.

1. **A: Where's / Who's** Martin?

   B: He's in Mexico City.

2. **A: How old / What time** is Penny?

   B: She's 15.

3. **A: When's / Where's** your birthday?

   B: May 16.

4. **A: Who / When** are your friends?

   B: Tim and Rita.

have, p. 25

Use have to talk about possessions, characteristics, and relationships.

Affirmative			Negative		
I	have	a brother.	I	don't have	a sister.
He/She/It	has	a big family.	He/She/It	doesn't have	a small family.
You/We/They	have	a big house.	You/We/They	don't have	a small house.

Yes/No questions			Short answers					
Do	I	have a brother?	Yes,	you	do.	No,	you	don't.
Do	you	have a sister?		I	do.		I	don't.
Does	he/she/it	have a big family?		he/she/it	does.		he/she/it	doesn't.
Do	we/they	have a big house?		we/they	do.		we/they	don't.

1. **Complete the conversations with the correct form of *have* or short answers.**

    1. **A:** _____ Jason _____ a brother?
       B: No, he _____. But he _____ two sisters.
    2. **A:** _____ you _____ a big house?
       B: Yes, I _____. It _____ six bedrooms! But I _____ a big yard. The yard is really small.
    3. **A:** _____ Martin and Veronica _____ jobs?
       B: No, they _____. They're only 10 and 12 years old!
    4. **A:** _____ Wanda _____ a big family?
       B: Yes, _____. She _____ seven brothers, but she _____ a sister.

Comparative adjectives, p. 27

Use comparative adjectives to show how two things are different from each other.

1 syllable	dark → dark**er** nice → nic**er** big → big**ger**	My hair is **darker than** his hair. James is **nicer than** Megan. My brother is **bigger than** your brother.
2 or more syllables	intelligent → **more** intelligent	My avatar is **more intelligent** than your avatar.
Ending in consonant + -y	wavy → wav**ier**	It's **wavier than** your hair.
Irregular	good → **better** bad → **worse**	Ahmed's avatar is **better than** my avatar. My avatar is **worse than** his avatar.

2. **Write sentences with comparative adjectives.**

    1. Yoli / old / her sister _____
    2. Mark / tall / Ben _____
    3. My hair / curly / my mom's hair _____
    4. Oliver / handsome / his brother _____
    5. My avatar / bad / your avatar _____

Simple present statements, p. 35

Use the present simple to talk about routines, habits, and facts.

Affirmative			Negative		
I/You	**start**	classes at 8:00 a.m.	I/You	**don't start**	classes at 9:00 a.m.
He/She/It	**starts**		He/She/It	**doesn't start**	
We/You/They	**start**		We/You/They	**don't start**	

Affirmative			Negative		
I/You	**go**	to school.	I/You	**don't go**	to school.
He/She/It	**goes**		He/She/It	**doesn't go**	
We/You/They	**go**		We/You/They	**don't go**	

| Contractions | do not = **don't** | | does not = **doesn't** | |

1. Complete the sentences with the correct affirmative or negative forms of the verbs.

brush   exercise   get   take   sleep

1. I _don't exercise_ at the gym, but I play soccer in the park.
2. You _____ a shower every evening. You always go to bed clean!
3. My grandfather _____ his hair because he's bald. He doesn't have hair!
4. Brittany _____ up at 7:00 every morning because she starts school at 8:00.
5. Sammy and his father _____ late on weekends. They get up early and have breakfast together.

Simple present questions, p. 37

Ask yes/no questions to get short, simple affirmative or negative responses about routines, habits, and facts. Ask Wh- questions to get more specific information.

Yes/No questions				Short answers					
Do	I	**play** sports?	Yes,	you	do.	No,	you	don't.
Do	you			I	do.		I	don't.
Does	he/she/it			he/she/it	does.		he/she/it	doesn't.
Do	we/you/they			we/you/they	do.		we/you/they	don't.

Wh- questions			
Who What Where When Why How	do	I/you/we/they	**play** . . . ?
	does	he/she/it	

2. Complete the questions. Match the questions with the correct answers.

1. ___Does___ she listen to the radio? _d_
2. Where _____ Todd and Sue go swimming? ___
3. How often do you _____ art classes? ___
4. Do _____ do drama? ___
5. What kind of dance classes _____ Carla take? ___

a. They usually go to the town pool.
b. Yes, we do. We act at the local theater.
c. She takes tango lessons.
d. No, she doesn't
e. I take them once a week.

can for ability, p. 45

Affirmative		Negative	
I/he/she/it/you/we/they	can do kung fu.	I/he/she/it/you/we/they	can't do karate.
	can break a brick.		can't break a brick.
Questions		**Answers**	
Can I/he/she/it/you/we/they break a brick?		Yes, I/he/she/it/you/we/they can.	
What can I/he/she/it/you/we/they do?		No, I/he/she/it/you/we/they can't.	
		I/he/she/it/you/we/they can do a lot of moves.	
Contraction cannot = can't			

Use can to express what someone or something is able or not able to do.

1. **Rewrite the sentences and questions with can or can't.**

   1. Leslie sings well. *Leslie can sing well.*
   2. Mike doesn't play the guitar. _____
   3. Do you play basketball? _____
   4. What does she play? _____
   5. We don't dance at all. _____
   6. Mateo and Emma speak English and Spanish. _____

Object pronouns; verb + -ing form (gerund) for opinions, p. 47

Use object pronouns to replace nouns that follow verbs. They receive the action of the verb.

Subject pronoun	I	he	she	it	you	we	they
Object pronoun	me	him	her	it	you	us	them

I love my dance class. → I love **it**.
Tom takes art classes in the morning. → He takes **them** in the morning.
They give homework to my classmates and me. → They give **it** to **us**.

Use -ing forms (gerunds) after certain verbs to express opinions. Use the object pronoun it to replace these -ing forms and phrases.

😃 love   🙂 like   😐 don't mind   🙁 don't like   🤢 hate

Tom loves dancing. → He loves **it**.
I **don't mind** doing homework. → I don't mind **it**.
Do you **like** playing the guitar? → Do you like **it**?

2. **Rewrite the sentences with object pronouns for the underlined words.**

   1. When do you take art classes? _____
   2. Please give the laptop to Laura. _____
   3. I hate playing the violin! _____
   4. Do you like studying Spanish? _____
   5. We see Mr. Moore on Tuesdays. _____
   6. Please show the pictures to Wayne and me. _____

This page intentionally left blank.

Percentages and PIE CHARTS

CLIL PROJECT

1. A *percentage* can be a small or large part of a whole thing. The *whole* equals 100% (one hundred percent). What percentage of each pie chart is blue? Label the pictures with the correct percentages.

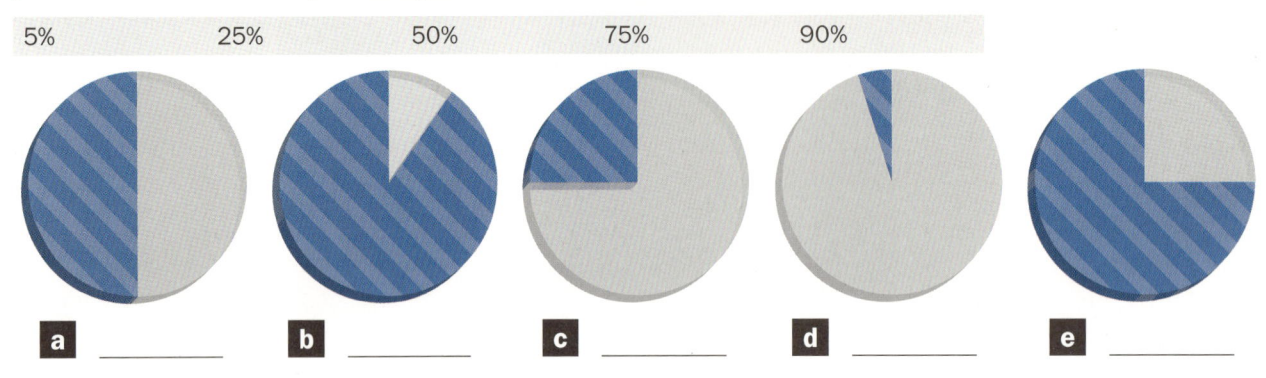

   5%   25%   50%   75%   90%

   a _____   b _____   c _____   d _____   e _____

2. Match the sentences with the pie charts from Exercise 1.

   1. **Almost all** of the people in Mexico speak Spanish. _b_
   2. **Around half** of all South Americans live in Brazil. ____
   3. **A small portion** of Americans work in finance. ____
   4. **About one-quarter** of the population of Japan is over 64 years old. ____
   5. **Three-quarters** of Colombians live in cities. ____

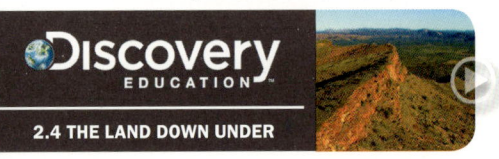

Discovery EDUCATION
2.4 THE LAND DOWN UNDER

3. Watch the video. Complete the summary with the correct percentages.

   10%   25%   33%   75%   80%   80%   90%

   In "The Land Down Under," [1]_____ of the population speaks English. However, [2]_____ of the population is from other countries. Many people, [3]_____ of the population, live in cities. About [4]_____ of the population lives near the ocean. An important industry is mining. About [5]_____ of the people in the country work in mines. The land and the animals are special, too. About [6]_____ of the country is desert, and about [7]_____ of the animals do not live anywhere else in the world!

PROJECT Choose a country. Answer the questions and create a poster with the information. Include a map, the flag, and pie charts to show your percentages. Present your poster to the class.

- What are two cities in the country? What percentage of the population lives in each city?
- What languages do people speak? What percentage of the population speaks the top two or three languages?
- What are two other interesting facts about the population or the country?

In OUR SOLAR SYSTEM

1. **Complete the paragraph. Use the correct forms of the words in the picture.**

   Our solar system has eight [1]_____. They [2]_____ around the Sun. Our planet is Earth. It is the only planet in our solar system with people on it. Earth is called the "Blue Planet" because it has a lot of water in lakes, rivers, and oceans. Earth also has high [3]_____, deep [4]_____, and dry [5]_____. One day is the time a planet takes to [6]_____ on its [7]_____. One day on Earth is 24 hours. One year is the time a planet takes to go around the Sun. One year on Earth is 365 days. Some planets have many [8]_____ that revolve around them, but Earth only has one. Our Blue Planet is very interesting.

2. **Watch the video. Complete the information about Mars.**

Name of planet	Earth	Mars	
Order from the Sun	3rd	4th	
Length of one day	24 hours		
Length of one year	365.25 days		
Number of moons	1		
Features	mountains deserts valleys lakes rivers oceans		
Other interesting information	Earth is the only planet in our solar system that has people on it! Earth is called the "Blue Planet". The surface of Earth is 70% water.		

PROJECT Research another planet in our solar system. Complete the third column of the chart and present your information to the class. Use pictures in your presentation.

This page intentionally left blank.

Uncover 1 Combo A

Susan Evento

Workbook

CAMBRIDGE UNIVERSITY PRESS

Discovery EDUCATION

1 Welcome Back!

VOCABULARY Classroom objects and colors

1 Circle nine more classroom objects.

chair board notebook pencil bookshelf (dictionary) eraser ruler backpack book

2 Complete the sentences with color words.

1. Black + white = _____gray_____
2. Red + blue = _____
3. Blue + yellow = _____
4. Red + yellow = _____
5. Red + yellow + blue = _____

3 Complete the sentences with color words.

1. The American flag is red, white, and _____blue_____.

2. The sun is a big _____ ball.

3. Most soccer balls are _____ and white.

4. The angry boy's face is _____.

5. Snow is _____.

4 Answer the questions.

1. What color is your notebook?
   _____My notebook is black._____

2. What color is your pencil?
   _____

3. What color are your eyes?
   _____

4. What colors are your schoolbooks?
   _____

5. What color are your shoes?
   _____

6. What color is your backpack?
   _____

GRAMMAR Simple present of *be* and subject pronouns

1 Circle the correct simple present forms of *be*.

1. I **is** / **am** a good photographer.
2. He **is** / **am** a new student.
3. They **is** / **are** good friends.
4. It **is** / **are** Tuesday.
5. We **are** / **is** at the store.
6. She **am** / **is** happy it is Friday.
7. You **are** / **is** next in line.
8. Brett and Jim **is** / **are** football players.
9. The band **are** / **is** playing.
10. That team **is** / **are** the best.

2 Complete the sentences with the correct pronouns.

1. Betty is in the band. _____She_____ isn't a dancer.
2. My friend and I are in middle school. _____ aren't in high school.
3. Brian and Justin are in different grades. _____ aren't in the same classes.
4. The dictionary is on the bookshelf. _____ isn't on the desk.
5. Jim is in the library. _____ isn't in the cafeteria.

3 Complete the chart. Use contractions.

	Affirmative	Negative	Question
I	I am in this class.	I'm not in this class.	
He		He isn't angry.	
She			Is she a musician?
It		It isn't a nice day.	
You	You are at the party.		
We			Are we early for the show?
They		They aren't home now.	

4 Correct the verbs.

1. They ~~is~~ *are* in the same class.
2. Are he on the football team?
3. I is not angry with you.
4. John and I am best friends.
5. It am Tuesday.
6. The team are at the field.
7. What are his favorite class?
8. Who is your classmates?

5 Answer the questions.

1. How old are you?
   _____
2. Who are your best friends?
   _____
3. Are you on a team? What team?
   _____
   _____
4. What is your favorite color?
   _____
5. Who are your favorite bands?
   _____

VOCABULARY Instructions

1 Put the letters in the correct order to make words.

1. AERD ____read____
2. RNTU _____
3. MCOE _____
4. PONE _____
5. SEAIR _____
6. TISENL _____
7. SATND _____
8. OSLCE _____
9. IST _____

2 Write the instructions under the pictures. Use the verbs. Some instructions use nouns.

Verbs	Nouns
be quiet	~~the article~~
close	the book
open	the door
~~read~~	your name
sit down	
stand up	
write	

1. __Read the article.__   2. _____

3. _____   4. _____

5. _____   6. _____

3 Write three more instructions. Use words from Exercises 1 and 2.

1. _____Open the window._____
2. _____
3. _____
4. _____

4 Where do you hear the instructions? Circle the correct answers.

1. Open your book.
   a. at home
   b. at school
   c. at the gym

2. Be quiet.
   a. in the cafeteria
   b. in the library
   c. in the park

3. Raise your hand.
   a. at home
   b. in the park
   c. in the classroom

4. Listen to the teacher.
   a. at school
   b. at home
   c. on the football field

5. Turn to page 12.
   a. in the gym
   b. in the cafeteria
   c. in the classroom

6. Close the window.
   a. at home
   b. on the football field
   c. in the park

4 | Unit 1

GRAMMAR Imperatives

1 Correct the sentences.

HOUSEHOLD RULES

1. Leave your clothes on the floor.
   Don't leave your clothes on the floor.

2. Be loud at the dinner table.
   _____

3. Don't get up when your alarm rings in the morning.
   _____

4. Don't go to bed early.
   _____

5. Fight with your brother and sister.
   _____

6. Don't do your homework.
   _____

7. Play soccer in the house.
   _____

8. Don't turn off the lights when you leave the room.
   _____

2 Rewrite the sentences. Use *please* to make the commands softer. Remember, *please* can go at the beginning or end of a sentence.

1. Don't go in the street.
   Please don't go in the street. OR
   Don't go in the street, please.

2. Don't say that again.
   _____

3. Sit down.
   _____

4. Take turns.
   _____

5. Look at this.
   _____

6. Don't write in the book.
   _____

7. Be quiet in the library.
   _____

8. Don't eat in class.
   _____

3 Complete the sentences with imperatives.

| be | listen | raise | stand |
| eat | open | sit | turn |

1. ____*Eat*____ your vegetables. They are good for you.
2. _____ the window to let air in.
3. _____ your hand to talk.
4. Please _____ to what I say.
5. It's dark. _____ the light on.
6. Don't _____ on the desk.
7. Don't _____ on the chairs. It's dangerous.
8. Please _____ on time for class.

Unit 1 | 5

CONVERSATION — That's my name!

1 Put the words in the correct order to make questions or sentences. Then complete the conversation.

do / say / that word / How / you /

repeat / Can / that / you /

does / mean / that word / what /

understand / don't / I /

Juan: Hey, Marisa.

Marisa: Hey, Juan. Look at this book.

¹ *How do you say that word* ?

Juan: "Board."

Marisa: ² _____ slowly, please?

Juan: Sure. "Board."

Marisa: Thanks, but ³ _____ ?

Juan: It's something the teacher writes on.

Marisa: Huh? ⁴ _____ .

Juan: Ms. Wilson writes our lessons on the board.

Marisa: Oh. Now I understand! Thanks. I like to learn new words.

2 Use the words to complete the conversation. There are two extra words.

How	repeat	understand
mean	say	What

Luc: Hey, Juan.

Juan: Hi, Luc.

Luc: ¹ _____ do you say *bonjour* in English?

Juan: *Hello.*

Luc: I don't ² _____ . How do you spell it?

Juan: H-E-L-L-O.

Luc: Can you ³ _____ that, please?

Juan: Sure. H-E-L-L-O.

Luc: Oh, *hello*. Thanks.

Juan: Hey, Luc. What does *notebook* ⁴ _____ ?

Luc: Oh, I know that word. It's a book you write in.

Juan: I need to buy one of those.

READING TO WRITE

1 Match the pictures with the sentences. Then add one Do rule to the list and one Don't rule.

POOL RULES
Dos and Don'ts

POOL RULES: DOS AND DON'TS

Do . . .

1. ___b___ Wear a bathing cap.

2. _____ Be safe on the diving board!

3. _____ Take a shower before you go in the pool.

4. _____

Don't . . .

1. _____ Don't play loud music.

2. _____ Don't run!

3. _____ Don't eat or drink in the pool.

4. _____

2 Read the instructions for riding a bike. Add missing periods and exclamation points.

1. Wear a helmet

2. Use lights at night

3. Hold the handlebars

4. Look both ways before you turn

5. Stop at the red light

3 Think of a game or activity that has important rules. Write four Do rules and four Don't rules. Write the most important rules first. Add periods or exclamation points.

Dos	Don'ts

Unit 1 | 7

2 My World

VOCABULARY Personal items

1 Complete the crossword puzzle.

Down
1. 
2. 
4. 
5. 
7. 
8.

Across
3. 
6. 
7. 
9. 
10. 
11.

2 Look at Selena Gomez's favorite things. Complete her profile with the correct words.

comic books
soccer
guitar
tablet
sneakers

My Favorite Things

by Selena

Favorite sport: _____soccer_____

Favorite technology: _____

Favorite things to read: _____

Favorite instrument: _____

Favorite shoes: _____

3 Complete the sentences with the correct words.

guitar	skateboard
inline skates	soccer ball
laptop	tablet
~~MP3 player~~	sneakers

1. We use an ____MP3 player____ and a _____ to play music.

2. A _____ and a _____ are types of computers.

3. People wear _____ and _____ on their feet.

4. Paul likes to kick a _____, but John likes to ride a _____.

8 | Unit 2

GRAMMAR Possessives

1 Complete the sentences with possessive adjectives.

Subject pronouns	Possessive adjectives
I	I like _____my_____ pink hat.
you	Eat _____ vegetables.
he	He meets _____ mother at the store.
she	She plays _____ favorite song.
it	See that lake? _____ name is Lake Erie.
we	We eat _____ lunch together on Fridays.
you	Please tell me _____ names.
they	Jan and Kim meet _____ friends at the store.

2 Complete the sentences with possessive adjectives.

1. My family has a cat. _____Our_____ cat's name is Josie.
2. Carlos is from Italy. _____ family is from Rome.
3. Two students in the class don't have _____ homework.
4. We have many students in _____ school.
5. That dress is very pretty. _____ colors are beautiful.
6. You have to do _____ homework!

3 Rewrite the sentences. Use possessive adjectives.

1. The students' teacher is very nice!
   _____Their teacher is very nice!_____
2. Stephanie's parents are doctors.
   _____
3. Dave talks to Dave's grandmother on the phone every week.
   _____
4. Shawn and my friend is from Ireland.
   _____
5. Caroline's brothers and sisters are in a band.
   _____

4 Complete the sentences with possessive adjectives or name/noun + 's or s'.

Laia   Alicia

Hector   Sergio

1. _____Laia's_____ favorite thing is _____her_____ cat, Chester.
2. _____ favorite thing is _____ game console.
3. _____ favorite thing is _____ guitar.
4. _____ favorite things are _____ books.

5 Circle the correct words.

1. The **boy's** / **(boys')** names **is** / **are** James and Connor.
2. The two **girl's** / **girls'** favorite game **is** / **are** soccer.
3. My **teacher's** / **teachers'** names **is** / **are** Mr. Kent and Ms. Childs.
4. The **truck's** / **trucks'** engine **is** / **are** loud.
5. All of the **student's** / **students'** papers **is** / **are** interesting.

6 Correct the sentences.

1. My brothers name is Sam.
   _____My brother's name is Sam._____
2. Lauras favorite color is red.
   _____
3. Carlos loves its cat.
   _____
4. The cars colors are black and blue.
   _____
5. We do her homework together.
   _____

Unit 2 | 9

VOCABULARY Countries, nationalities, and languages

1 Put the letters in the correct order to make words.

1. GUORPTEESU ___Portuguese___
2. GISHLEN _____
3. ISHANSP _____
4. ALITIAN _____
5. IABRZILAN _____
6. NEIXMCA _____
7. DIAANNAC _____
8. SEPAJANE _____

2 Match the countries with the nationalities.

1. Japan — a. Mexican
2. Australia — b. British
3. Brazil — c. Australian
4. Mexico — d. Brazilian
5. the UK — e. French
6. France — f. Japanese

3 Complete the sentences with the correct languages.

1. Spanish people speak ___Spanish___.
2. Canadians speak English and _____.
3. Sudanese people speak English and _____.
4. Australians speak _____.
5. Brazilians speak _____.
6. British people speak _____.
7. In Colombia, people speak _____.
8. In Italy, people speak _____.

4 Write the nationalities and languages.

Penelope Cruz   Taylor Swift

Robert Pattinson   Keith Urban

Cristiano Ronaldo   Sofia Vegara

1. Penelope Cruz is from Spain. She's ___Spanish___. She speaks _____.
2. Taylor Swift is from America. She's _____. She speaks _____.
3. Robert Pattinson is from the U.K. He's _____. He speaks _____.
4. Keith Urban is from Australia. He's _____. He speaks _____.
5. Cristiano Ronaldo is from Portugal. He's _____. He speaks _____.
6. Sofia Vegara is from Colombia. She's _____. She speaks _____.

5 Choose three people. Write sentences about their nationalities and the languages they speak.

1. _____
2. _____
3. _____

GRAMMAR Question words

1 Read the paragraph. Then circle the correct question words. Answer the questions.

> Juan lives in Puerto Rico. He goes to Antilles Middle School. Juan takes English, math, science, history, and computer lab. He has two best friends. They are Luis and Edwin. On Fridays, they walk or ride their bicycles to the park. They play baseball at the park. It is their favorite sport.

1. **How** / **(Where)** does Juan live?
   He lives in Puerto Rico.

2. **Where** / **What** does he go to school?
   _____

3. **What** / **Where** are his classes in school?
   _____

4. **How** / **Who** are his best friends?
   _____

5. **When** / **Where** do they go to the park?
   _____

6. **What** / **How** do the boys get to the park?
   _____

7. **When** / **What** sport do the boys play at the park?
   _____

2 Fill in the correct question words. Then answer the questions.

1. ____What____ is your name?
   _____

2. _____ do you live?
   _____

3. _____ old are you?
   _____

4. _____ is your birthday?
   _____

5. _____ class are you in?
   _____

6. _____ do you get to school?
   _____

7. _____ are your favorite things to do?
   _____

8. _____ are your favorite classes?
   _____

3 Read the answers. Write the questions.

Hello, my name is Asako!

1. _____Where are you from?_____
   I'm from Tokyo, Japan.

2. _____
   My best friends are Kameko and Nami.

3. _____
   My English teacher is Mr. Smith.

4. _____
   My favorite thing is my MP3 player!

CONVERSATION   Meeting and greeting

1 Put the sentences in order to make a conversation.

Marty: Hello! My name is Marty. What's your name?

Marty: Nice to meet you, too.

Josh: Are you the new player on our soccer team?

Marty: Yes, I am.

Marty: Thanks! Hey, I've got class. See you on the soccer field. Bye!

Josh: That's great. Welcome to the team.

Josh: Hi. My name's Josh. Nice to meet you.

2 Circle the correct words.

1. **(This)** / **That** is my mother next to me. **These** / **Those** are her friends Mr. and Mrs. Miller right next to her.

2. **That** / **This** is my brother on the soccer field. And **these** / **those** are his friends with him.

3. Come meet one of my best friends. **This** / **That** is Marcia.

4. **These** / **Those** people near the door are Marcia's family.

READING TO WRITE

1 Read Amaris Moreno's profile. Complete the chart.

> My name is Amaris Moreno. I'm Colombian and I'm from Bogotá. I live with my mom and dad. We all speak English and Spanish.
>
> I am 11 years old. My birthday is in just a few days, on April 15. I can't wait for my party with my favorite music and food. I love rap music and pizza.
>
> My favorite thing to do is play my guitar. I also like to write stories and play games on my new tablet.

Name	Birthday / Age
Amaris Moreno	
Town / City	**Country**
Nationality	**Languages**
Likes	**Interests**

2 Correct the incorrect words. Add capital letters. Then use the words to write four sentences about Adriano.

1. Adriano ~~s~~Silva, são Paulo, brazil

   His name is Adriano Silva, and he lives in São Paulo, Brazil.

2. brazilian, Portuguese

   _____.

3. Birthday: may 3

   _____

4. Favorite soccer player: victor andrade

   _____

Unit 2 | 13

REVIEW UNITS 1–2

1 Label each object. Then circle the classroom words.

board	game console	ruler
comic books	inline skates	skateboard
dictionary	notebook	soccer ball
eraser	pencil	

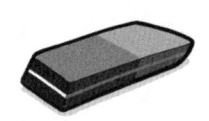

1. _____
2. _____ 
3. _____ 
4. _____ 
5. _____ 
6. _____ 
7. _____ 
8. _____ 
9. _____ 
10. _____ 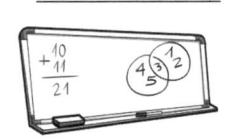
11. _____ 

2 Fill in the correct words.

1. Jason is from Australia. He is _____.
   He speaks _____.

2. Elena is from _____. She is Brazilian.
   She speaks _____.

3. Mateo is from Spain. He is _____.
   He speaks _____.

4. Samir is from Sudan. He is _____.
   He speaks _____ and English.

5. Amaya is from Japan. She is _____.
   She speaks _____.

6. Eduardo is from Colombia. He is _____.
   He speaks _____.

3 Complete the sentences with the correct form of *be*.

1. The pencil _____ yellow.
2. John and Pat _____ in my class.
3. Our school band _____ new.
4. I _____ a football player on our school team.
5. Tryouts _____ tomorrow.
6. The ruler and the eraser _____ pink.

4 Make the sentences in Exercise 3 negative. Use subject pronouns for names and objects. Use contractions.

1. _____*It isn't yellow.*_____
2. _____
3. _____
4. _____
5. _____
6. _____

5 Complete the class rules handout with the imperative form of the verbs.

| be | open | read | sit |
| come | raise | run | talk |

Welcome to
AMERICAN HISTORY!
Please follow this list of class rules.

Dos:
1. _____ your hand in class. Questions are good!
2. _____ on time. Class starts at 1:30.
3. _____ to every class.
4. _____ your book for homework.

Don'ts:
1. _____ in the hall.
2. _____ when your teacher or classmates are talking.
3. _____ on your desk. Use your chair.
4. _____ your books during tests.

6 Use a possessive adjective or a name/noun + 's or s' for plural subjects.

1. (Lily) _____ game console is _____ favorite thing.
2. (Anuj) _____ favorite thing is _____ dog, Rusty.
3. The (girls) _____ favorite things are _____ MP3 players.
4. The new (students) _____ names are Zack and Ian, and _____ teacher is Mrs. Lucas.

7 Ask and answer questions about Pedro.

Pedro's Personal Profile

Name	Pedro Alonzez
Age	12
Birthday	4/15
Nationality	Colombian
Town/City	Bogotá
Country	Colombia
Language(s)	Spanish
Interests/Favorite things	Soccer, rap music

1. **A:** _____
   B: He lives in Bogotá, Colombia.
2. **A:** _____
   B: Pedro is 12 years old.
3. **A:** What is Pedro's favorite sport?
   B: _____
4. **A:** What kind of music does Pedro like?
   B: _____
5. **A:** What language does Pedro speak?
   B: _____
6. **A:** _____
   B: It is April 15.

8 Complete the meeting and greeting conversations with the words in the box.

fine   problem
later   welcome
meet   what's
name   you

1. **A:** My _____ is Alex. _____ your name?
   B: I'm Paola.
2. **A:** Nice to _____ you!
   B: Nice to meet you, too!
3. **A:** Where are you from?
   B: I'm from the USA. And what about _____?
4. **A:** How are you?
   B: _____ thanks, and you?
5. **A:** Thanks for your help!
   B: No _____. You're _____.
6. **A:** See you at 3:00.
   B: See you _____.

9 Put the words in the correct order to ask questions about learning a new language. Then match the questions to the answers.

1. please / repeat / that / you / Can / ?
   _____
   _____

2. spell / do / English / in / you / How / *diccionario* / ?
   _____
   _____

3. don't / I / understand /.
   _____
   _____

4. mean / What / it / does / ?
   _____
   _____

   a. I'll try to explain.
   b. It is a book that tells you what words mean.
   c. D-I-C-T-I-O-N-A-R-Y
   d. Yes, the word is *dictionary*.

3 People in My Life

VOCABULARY Family and friends

1 Look at the family tree. Circle the correct family words.

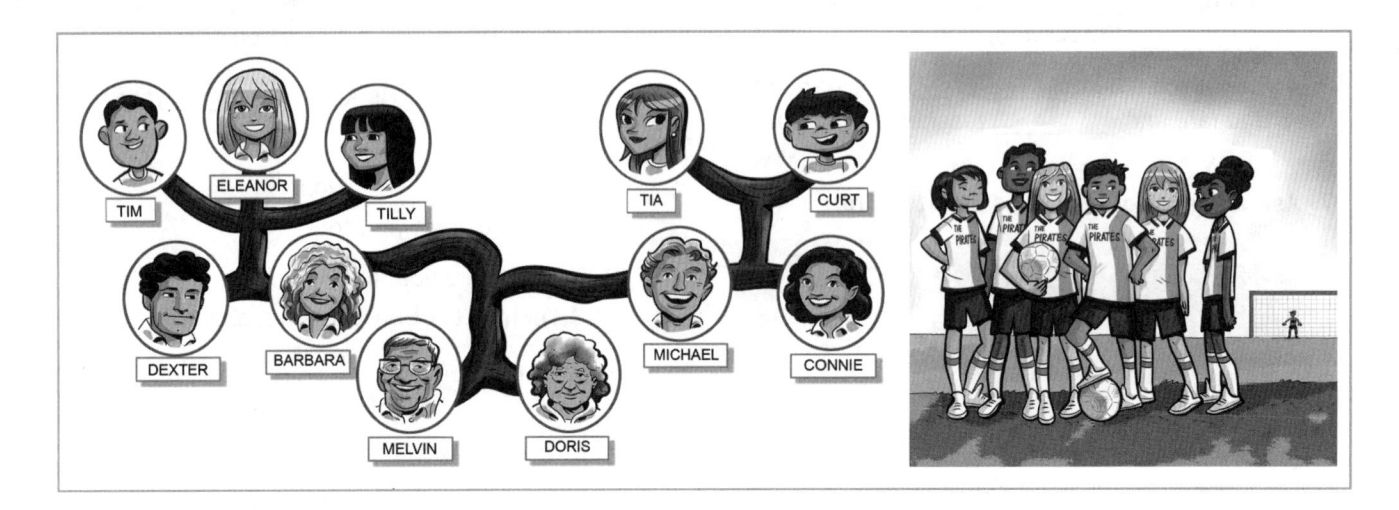

1. Barbara is Eleanor's **mother** / **aunt**.
2. Tia and Curt are her **parents** / **cousins**.
3. Melvin is her **uncle** / **grandfather**.
4. Michael is her **cousin** / **uncle**.
5. Connie is her **sister** / **aunt**.
6. Eleanor is Melvin's and Doris's **son** / **granddaughter**.
7. Dexter and Barbara are her **parents** / **grandparents**.
8. "The Pirates" are Eleanor's **classmates** / **teammates**.

2 Find 12 more words for friends and family.

S	T	T	R	M	Y	P	W	D	A	T	N	F
E	A	N	C	O	U	S	I	N	T	E	K	O
F	H	U	L	T	U	B	N	R	Q	A	R	N
I	F	A	T	H	E	R	O	E	S	M	A	Y
W	P	S	N	E	W	O	J	T	J	M	W	A
F	N	G	W	R	N	T	Y	S	X	A	G	C
H	W	S	P	X	D	H	H	I	M	T	D	K
U	N	C	L	E	U	E	Y	S	Y	E	H	F
S	U	N	T	P	A	R	E	N	T	S	I	O
B	L	C	L	A	S	S	M	A	T	E	S	P
A	Z	X	C	V	B	N	L	K	J	H	G	F
N	G	R	A	N	D	P	A	R	E	N	T	S
D	Q	W	E	R	T	U	I	O	P	A	S	D

3 Use the words to write sentences about your family.

aunt	grandfather
brother	grandmother
classmates	mother
cousin	sister
father	uncle

1. _My sister Carol is twelve._
2. _____
3. _____
4. _____
5. _____
6. _____

GRAMMAR *have*

1 Complete the chart.

John's FAMILY	
Affirmative	**Negative**
1. I ___*have*___ three brothers.	I _____ any sisters.
2. My cousin Janet _____ two sisters.	My cousin Janet _____ any brothers.
3. My grandparents _____ six children.	They _____ a small family.
4. My brother Jack _____ a cat named Max.	He _____ a pet snake.
5. My mother and father _____ big family parties.	They _____ small family parties.

2 Circle the correct form of *have*.

1. John **has / have** a cousin named Janet.
2. John and his brothers **don't have / don't has** any sisters.
3. John's brother Jack **don't has / doesn't have** a pet snake.
4. John **has / have** lots of aunts and uncles.

3 Answer the questions.

1. Does John have a baby sister?

   ___*No, John doesn't have a baby sister.*___

2. Do John and Jack have a big family?

   _____

3. Do John's parents have family parties?

   _____

4. Does John's brother Jack have a cat?

   _____

5. Does John's cousin Janet have any brothers?

   _____

4 Write sentences about you. Use *have* or *don't have*.

1. Cell phone?

   ___*I don't have a cell phone.*___

2. Comic books?

   _____

3. Game console?

   _____

4. Soccer ball?

   _____

5. Inline skates?

   _____

6. Guitar?

   _____

7. Big family?

   _____

Unit 3 | **17**

VOCABULARY Describing people

1 Match the pictures with the correct descriptions. Write a sentence for each.

1 Eduardo	2 Tammy	3 Jessie	4 Erica
_____	*Tammy has short, light wavy hair.*	_____	_____

a. short, light wavy hair
b. long, dark straight hair
c. short, dark curly hair
d. long, dark curly hair

2 Draw two people in the boxes. Give them names. Then write a sentence describing each one.

Name: _____
_____
_____

Name: _____
_____
_____

3 Write five sentences describing a good friend or someone in your family.

1. *My friend Leah is very funny and really intelligent.*
2. _____
3. _____
4. _____
5. _____
6. _____

18 | Unit 3

GRAMMAR Comparative adjectives

Cathy   Brad   Jake

1 Circle the correct answers.

1. Cathy is (younger) / **more younger** than Brad and Jake.
2. Cathy is **shorter / more short** than Brad and Jake.
3. Cathy's hair is **curly / curlier** than Jake's hair.
4. Brad is **taller / more tall** than Cathy and Jake.
5. Jake is **older / more old** than Cathy.
6. Brad's hair is **darker / more dark** than Cathy's hair.

2 Write four sentences about Cathy, Brad, and Jake. Use comparative adjectives and *than*.

1. *Jake's hair is straighter than Cathy's hair.*
2. _____
3. _____
4. _____
5. _____

3 Complete the paragraph with comparative adjectives and *than*.

Jackie and her friend Stella are very different. Jackie is
¹ _____*taller than*_____ (tall) Stella, and her hair
is ² _____ (dark) Stella's hair.
Stella is ³ _____ (short) Jackie,
and her hair is ⁴ _____ (wavy)
Jackie's hair. Stella thinks she is ⁵ _____
(funny) Jackie, but they are both very funny!

4 Complete the chart with the correct pronouns.

Possessive adjectives	Possessive pronouns
my	*mine*
_____	yours
his	_____
_____	hers
our	_____
their	_____

5 Correct the possessive adjectives and possessive pronouns.

1. ~~Mine~~ *My* hair is curlier than ~~you~~ *yours*.
2. You hair is longer than my.
3. His hair is wavier than their.
4. Our sister is older than yours sister.
5. Hers brother's eyes are bluer than your.
6. He is more intelligent than hers brother.

Unit 3 | 19

CONVERSATION   Talk to you soon.

1 Match the questions with the answers.

1. Hi, Paul. How are you?
2. Sorry, can I call you back?
3. Can you hold on a minute?
4. Do you have Jordan's email?
5. What's Jordan's phone number?

a. Sure. I'm not busy.
b. It's 980-555-2535.
c. I'm fine. How are you?
d. OK. I'll wait.
e. It's jb5@schoolemail.com.

2 Put the sentences in order to make a conversation.

_____ **Andrew:** I'm good, thanks. Hey, do you have John's phone number and email?

_____ **Amy:** Hold on a minute. Yes, here they are. His phone number is 825-555-9944. His email is johnw@online.com.

_____ **Amy:** Hi, Andrew. How are you?

_____ **Andrew:** Hi, Amy. It's Andrew.

___1___ **Amy:** Hello?

_____ **Amy:** I'll have to ask my parents. Can I call you back?

_____ **Andrew:** Sure. Call back soon, and we can make plans.

_____ **Andrew:** Thanks. I want to ask John to go to the movies tomorrow. Can you come, too?

READING TO WRITE

1 Circle the intensifiers.

1. David has blue eyes and is very tall and really handsome.
2. Their house is not very big, but it's really nice.
3. His father is very handsome, but he isn't very tall.
4. I love to read, but I'm not really interested in comic books.

2 Complete the word web with information about Justin Timberlake.

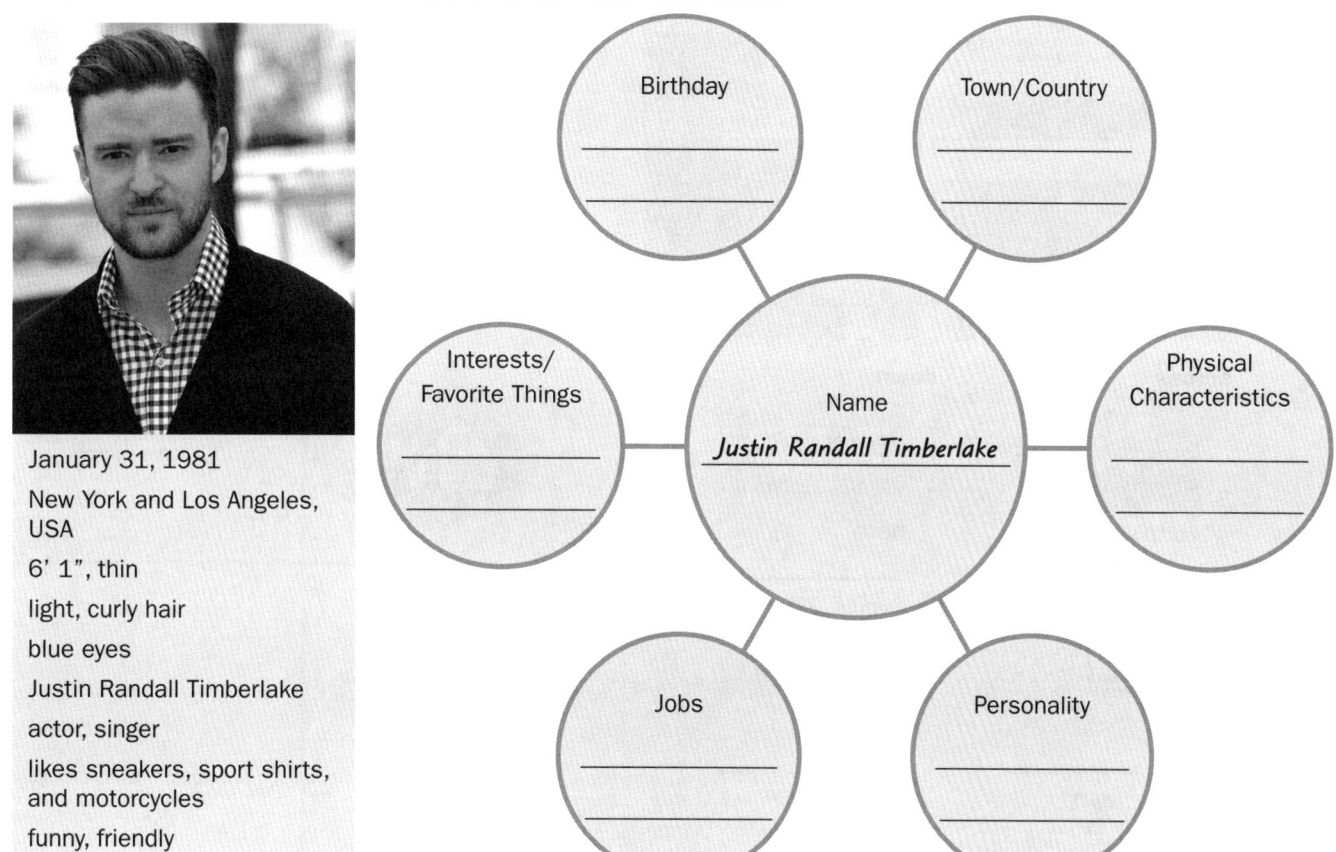

January 31, 1981
New York and Los Angeles, USA
6' 1", thin
light, curly hair
blue eyes
Justin Randall Timberlake
actor, singer
likes sneakers, sport shirts, and motorcycles
funny, friendly

- Birthday
- Town/Country
- Interests/Favorite Things
- Name: Justin Randall Timberlake
- Physical Characteristics
- Jobs
- Personality

3 Write four sentences about Justin Timberlake. Use intensifiers.

1. _Justin has very blue eyes._
2. _____
3. _____
4. _____
5. _____

4 It's My LIFE

VOCABULARY Daily routines

1 Complete the crossword.

```
        1
 2    ³b e d  4
 5
         6
 7
       8
```

across

3. go to _bed_
4. get _____ 
5. do some _____ 
6. start _____ 
7. do my _____ 
8. get _____ 

down

1. have _____
2. brush my _____ 
3. have _____ 
6. take a _____ 

2 Write the phrases from Exercise 1 in the order of your daily routine.

	have lunch

	have dinner
	go to bed

3 Choose four phrases from Exercise 2. Write sentences with your own information.

1. _I get up at 7:00 a.m._
2. _____
3. _____
4. _____
5. _____

22 | Unit 4

GRAMMAR Simple present statements

1 Circle the correct words.

1. You **go** / **goes** to school at 8:00 a.m.
2. He **finish** / **finishes** soccer at 6:00 p.m.
3. I **study** / **studies** very hard.
4. She **teach** / **teaches** Spanish.
5. They **play** / **plays** soccer after school.
6. We **do** / **does** our homework after school.
7. She **have** / **has** a big smile.

2 Write sentences from Exercise 1 and make them negative.

1. *You don't go to school at 8:00 a.m.*
2. _____
3. _____
4. _____
5. _____
6. _____
7. _____

3 Complete the sentences.

1. I _____ before the test.
2. We _____ lunch at noon.
3. My brother _____ soccer on the beach.
4. She _____ her homework every day.
5. You _____ at 6:30 a.m. every morning.
6. I _____ to school on the weekends.

4 Complete the text with the correct forms of the verbs.

Elias and Paul are eleven. They ¹____go____ (go) to a secondary school in Germany. They ²_____ (not wear) a uniform. They ³_____ (study) English, Latin, and 13 other subjects. They ⁴_____ (start) school at 7:30 a.m. and ⁵_____ (finish) classes at 1:30 p.m. Elias and Paul ⁶_____ (not have) lunch at school. Elias ⁷_____ (eat) at Paul's house with Paul's family. Elias's parents ⁸_____ (work) all day. After lunch, Paul and Elias ⁹_____ (play) sports. Sometimes Paul ¹⁰_____ (play) games while Elias ¹¹_____ (do) his chores. Then they both ¹²_____ (do) their homework.

5 Correct the sentences. One sentence is correct.

1. Eric ~~play~~ *plays* baseball on weekends.
2. We goes to a restaurant on Saturdays.
3. Cati do her homework in bed.
4. My cousins visits us for the holidays.
5. I get up early on Saturdays.
6. I shops for clothes with my parents.
7. My best friend watch football on TV.

Unit 4 | 23

VOCABULARY After-school activities

1 Put the letters in order to make after-school activities.

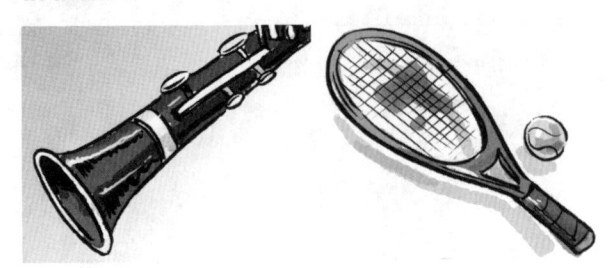

1. SUCIM — _music_
2. NETSIN — _____
3. SHECS — _____ 
4. GWINMISM — _____ 
5. RAT SECSALS — _____ 
6. ATAKER — _____ 
7. DENAC SEASLSC — _____ 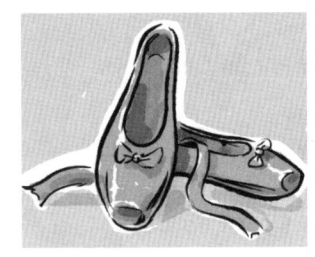
8. RAMAD — _____ 

2 Write the after-school activities from Exercise 1 in the correct columns.

Do	Go	Play	Take
		music	

3 Circle the activity that doesn't belong.

1. soccer
2. tennis
3. drama
4. swimming
5. karate

4 Write the activities in the correct columns.

art   drama   music   swimming
dance   karate   soccer   tennis

Arts	Sports
art	

GRAMMAR Simple present questions

1 Complete the chart with your own information. Write ✗ or ✓.

	Robert	Clara	_____
does karate	✗	✓	
goes swimming	✓	✓	
plays tennis	✗	✓	
takes dance classes	✗	✗	
takes art classes	✓	✗	
does drama	✓	✓	
plays music	✓	✗	

2 Write short answers to the questions. Use the information from the chart in Exercise 1.

1. Does Clara do karate?
   _____Yes, she does._____

2. Do Robert and Clara go swimming?
   _____

3. Does Robert play tennis?
   _____

4. Do Robert and Clara take dance classes?
   _____

5. Does Clara take art classes?
   _____

6. Do you do karate?
   _____

7. Do you play music?
   _____

3 Complete the sentences with the correct Wh- word.

1. __What__ music do you and your friends like?
   We like hip-hop music.

2. _____ do you go after school?
   We go to the park.

3. _____ do they go to the movies?
   They go on Saturday night.

4. _____ do you go to the movies with?
   I go with my best friend, Jessie.

5. _____ does your friend play the violin? She plays the violin because she likes classical music.

4 Complete the questions.

1. **A:** _____Do you eat_____ (you / eat) a lot of vegetables?
   B: Yes, I do.

2. **A:** _____ (your brother / play) the guitar?
   B: No, he doesn't.

3. **A:** _____ (Elias and Paul / finish) school at 1:30?
   B: Yes, they do.

4. **A:** _____ (you / like) comics, Paula?
   B: No, I don't.

5. **A:** _____ (you all / play) tennis at school?
   B: No, we don't.

5 Answer the questions with your own information. Use complete sentences.

1. Do you play basketball?
   _____Yes, I do. / No, I don't._____

2. Where do you go to school?
   _____

3. Do you play in the school band?
   _____

4. When do you go to bed?
   _____

5. What kind of music do you like?
   _____

Adverbs of frequency

Correct the adverbs of frequency. One sentence is correct.

usually
1. I get up ~~usually~~ early in the morning.

2. I play often tennis on the weekend.

3. I never am late to class.

4. I always am happy on Friday night.

5. I sometimes have lunch with my friend.

6. I go to bed late on the weekend usually.

CONVERSATION: I'd like some information, please.

1 Put the words in the correct order to make phrases for asking for information.

1. welcome / You're / .
   You're welcome.

2. close / does / time / What / the library / ?
   _____

3. days / the library / is / What / open / ?
   _____

4. a library card / you / Do / have / ?
   _____

5. can / How / you / I / help / ?
   _____

6. like / I'd / please / some information, / .
   _____

7. much / is / it / How / ?
   _____

2 Complete the conversation with phrases from Exercise 1.

Robin: Welcome to the Fairview Public Library! My name's Robin.
¹ _How can I help you?_

Dawn: Hi, Robin. ² _____ Do you have any books about Idina Menzel?

Robin: Yes, we do. They're in the biographies section.

Dawn: Great!

Robin: ³ _____

Dawn: No, I don't. ⁴ _____

Robin: The card is free, but there are late fees. It's $1 a day for DVDs and 25¢ a day for books.

Dawn: OK. ⁵ _____

Robin: It's open Monday through Saturday.

Dawn: ⁶ _____

Robin: It closes at 7:00.

Dawn: That's good. OK, I'll get a library card.

Robin: OK. Please write your name and address on this form. . . . Great! Here's your card.

Dawn: Perfect, thanks!

Robin: ⁷ _____ Have a nice day!

Dawn: Thanks, you too!

READING TO WRITE

1 Complete Blake's letter with *and*, *or*, or *but*.

Hi Blake,

My question is: What is your routine before the soccer world championships?

Marisol!

P.S. Good luck!

Hi Marisol,

Monday through Friday, I always get up at 6:00, ¹ __and__ I eat a big breakfast.

After dinner, around 8:00, I do my homework. I don't have a lot of free time, ² _____ sometimes I watch TV ³ _____ chat online with my friends.

I start school at 8:30 ⁴ _____ finish at 3:00.

I go to bed at 10:30.

I eat dinner at 7:15.

At 3:30 I run ⁵ _____ kick the soccer ball for three hours, so I get home at around 7:00.

On the weekends, I play soccer for four ⁶ _____ five hours, but on Saturday evening, I usually go to the movies or hang out with my friends.

Blake

2 Put the pieces of Blake's letter to Marisol in the correct order.

Hi Marisol,

Monday through Friday, I always get up at 6:00 _____ I eat a big breakfast.

_____

_____

_____

_____

_____

_____

_____

_____

_____

_____

_____

On weekends, I play soccer for four _____ five hours, but on Saturday evening, I usually go to the movies or hang out with my friends.

Blake

Unit 4 | 27

REVIEW UNITS 3–4

1 Look at the pictures of Eleanor's family and friends. Circle the correct words in the questions and write the answers.

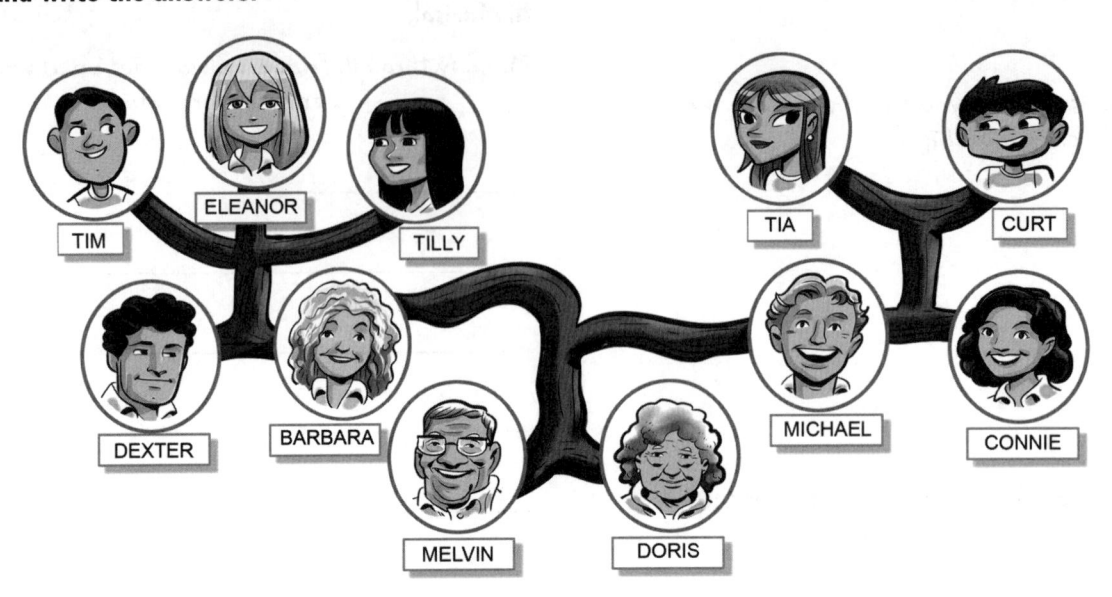

1. **(Does)** / **Do** Michael **have** / **has** white hair?
   No, he doesn't.

2. **Do** / **Does** Connie and Michael **have** / **has** wavy hair?
   _____

3. **Do** / **Does** Curt **have** / **has** a sister?
   _____

4. **Do** / **Does** Eleanor **have** / **has** a brother?
   _____

5. **Do** / **Does** Tim and Tilly **have** / **has** cousins?
   _____

2 Complete Eleanor's sentences.

curly	handsome	pretty
dark	intelligent	wavy
funny	light	young

1. My parents, Barbara and Dexter, have _____ hair.

2. My mom, Barbara, and I have _____ hair.

3. Aunt Connie and Uncle Michael have _____ hair.

4. My cousin, Tia, is good-looking. Tia is _____.

5. Uncle Michael is good-looking, too. Uncle Michael is _____.

6. My brother, Tim, knows a lot of things. He is _____.

7. My cousin, Curt, is only seven. He is _____.

3 Complete Timmy's daily routine. Use the words in the box.

always	goes	takes
arrives	never	usually
eats	sometimes	wakes

Every morning, Timmy ¹_____ up at 6:30. He ²_____ a shower every day at 7:00. He ³_____ does this at the same time. Most days, he ⁴_____ breakfast. After breakfast, Timmy ⁵_____ to school. He ⁶_____ walks to school, but other times he takes the bus. He ⁷_____ at school each morning at 8:00. He is ⁸_____ late. He ⁹_____ has Reading first, but on Fridays, he has Spanish first.

4 Complete the sentences.

1. Jill is _____ than Cindy.
2. Cindy is _____ Cheryl and Jill.
3. Cheryl's hair is _____ Cindy's hair.
4. Jill's hair is _____ Cheryl's hair.

5 Look at the pictures in Exercise 5. Complete the sentences.

1. Cindy _____ dance classes after school.
2. Jill _____ soccer on weekends.
3. Cheryl always _____ her homework.
4. Cheryl _____ very hard.

6 Complete the sentences with *always*, *usually*, *sometimes*, or *never*.

Jake	Michael	Kyle
Plays tennis every day from 3:00–5:00 p.m.	Plays tennis most Mondays and Wednesdays from 4:00–6:00 p.m. and most weekends	Plays tennis once in a while on Sundays

1. Michael _____ plays tennis on Tuesdays.
2. Jake _____ plays tennis from 3:00 to 5:00 p.m.
3. Kyle _____ plays tennis on Sundays.
4. Michael _____ plays tennis on the weekends.
5. Jake _____ plays tennis at 6:00 p.m.

7 Complete the phone conversation with the expressions. There is one extra expression.

call you back	How are you	Sure
Hi	It's	Talk to you soon
Hold on	jharris3@schoolemail.com	212-555-8927

Andrea: Hello?
Paul: Hi. ¹_____ Paul.
Andrea: ²_____, Paul.
Paul: ³_____?
Andrea: Good, thanks.
Paul: Hey, do you have Jason's cell phone number?
Andrea: Um, yes. ⁴_____ a minute. Okay, it's ⁵_____.
Paul: I want him to come over and play video games. Can you come over, too?
Andrea: When?
Paul: I don't know yet. Can I ⁶_____?
Andrea: ⁷_____.
Paul: Good. ⁸_____.

8 You want to take art classes. You call the Waterford Art Center. Look at the schedule and complete the questions.

Name of class	Day / Time	Room number	Price per class
Drawing Comics	Mon. and Wed. / 3:30 p.m.	Room 3	$5.00
Painting	Tues. and Thurs. / 5:00 p.m.	Room 6	$7.00
Computer Graphics	Sat. / 10:00 a.m.	Room 4	$5.00

1. What *are the names of the classes?*
   The names of the classes are Drawing Comics, Painting, and Computer Graphics.
2. When _____
   That class is on Monday and Wednesday at 3:30.
3. What _____
   It starts at 5:00 p.m.
4. Where _____
   That class is in Room 4.
5. How _____
   It costs $7.

5 School Days

VOCABULARY Places at School

1 Put the letters in the correct order to make words. Then write the name of each place under its picture.

DGAYRUPLNO _____
CSENICE BLA _____
BRLYARI _____
YMG _____
FTACEIRAE _____
RTA OORM _____
UDAMORTIUI _____
SMOSOLACR _____
NMIA FFICOE _____
PCUMRTEO ABL _____

1. _____
2. _____
3. _____
4. _____
5. _____
6. _____
7. _____
8. _____
9. _____
10. _____

2 Write each place from Exercise 1 in the correct column.

Places to study in school	Other places at school
	main office

3 Write sentences to tell what you do at the other places at school from Exercise 2.

1. *I go to the main office when I have questions about school.*
2. _____
3. _____
4. _____
5. _____

GRAMMAR *can* for ability

1 Complete the chart.

Affirmative	Negative
1. We / They / You ___can___ sing well.	2. We / They / You _____ sing well.
Questions	**Answers**
3. _____ I / he / she / it sing well?	4. Yes, I / he / she / it _____ sing well.
	5. No, I / he / she / it _____ sing well.

30 | Unit 5

2 Look at the pictures. Answer the questions using *can* and *can't*.

1. Can Vicky play the guitar?
   No, she can't.

2. Can Cathy do judo?
   _____

3. Can Alex sing?
   _____

4. Can Erin play tennis?
   _____

5. Can Mia play basketball?
   _____

6. Can Steven play the guitar?
   _____

3 Put the words in the correct order to ask questions. Then answer the questions with your own information.

1. talk / in / your / to / Can / your / friends / class / ?
   Can you talk to your friends in class?
   No, I can't. / Yes, I can.

2. you / Can / play / guitar / the / ?
   _____
   _____

3. you / speak / Can / Chinese / ?
   _____
   _____

4. ride / you / Can / horse / a / ?
   _____
   _____

5. kung fu / your / Can / do / mother / ?
   _____
   _____

6. can / songs / you / What / sing / ?
   _____
   _____

4 Complete the sentences with *can* or *can't*.

1. I just got new glasses. Now I ____*can*____ see the board.

2. Jason has a strong voice. He _____ sing very well.

3. Jessie has to babysit this weekend. She _____ come to my party on Saturday.

4. My legs aren't very strong. I _____ run very fast.

5. Terry is only 11. She _____ drive yet.

VOCABULARY School subjects

1 Find seven more school subjects.

✓civics	ICT
English	math
geography	PE
history	science

Q	W	E	R	T	Y	G	U	I
S	C	T	R	M	A	E	W	D
B	I	H	I	S	T	O	R	Y
F	V	U	L	B	O	G	K	S
A	I	F	P	E	C	R	O	E
I	C	T	N	C	M	A	T	H
F	S	G	W	V	N	P	Y	S
E	N	G	L	I	S	H	E	B
U	N	C	L	C	U	Y	Y	S
C	S	C	I	E	N	C	E	N

2 Write each word from Exercise 1 next to the correct picture.

1.  _____civics_____
2.  _____
3.  _____
4.  _____
5.  _____
6.  _____
7.  _____
8. _____

3 In which classes would you hear these questions? Write the school subjects.

1. "Where is Italy on a map?" _____geography_____
2. "What's 9 × 12?" _____
3. "How big is the sun?" _____
4. "Who was the first president of the United States of America?" _____
5. "What does *swim* mean?" _____
6. "How fast can you run?" _____

4 Correct the incorrect sentences. Write *correct* if no changes are needed.

1. Our class studies history in the cafeteria.
   Our class studies history in the classroom.

2. We have PE in the auditorium.
   _____

3. *ICT* means "Information Communication Technology."
   _____

4. *PE* means "Physical Exercise."
   _____

5. We have ICT in the science lab.
   _____

6. We study maps in math class.
   _____

5 Complete the sentences with your own information.

1. In PE _I can run faster than my classmates_.
2. In history we study _____.
3. In math class I _____.
4. I go to the library _____.
5. In science class we _____.
6. _____ is my favorite subject because _____.
7. _____ is my least favorite subject because _____.
8. In English class we can _____.

32 | Unit 5

GRAMMAR Object pronouns; verb + -ing form (gerund) for opinions

1 Underline the subject pronouns. Circle the object pronouns.

1. I am in an art class. I really like it.
2. My brother gives music lessons to my friends and me. He gives them to us for free.
3. Miss Grant gives books to Sophie, but she always reads them first.
4. Does Dina study French? Yes, she's very good at it.
5. Do Sherrell and Ivy take karate lessons? Yes, they take them on weekends.
6. Sonya usually kicks the ball to Wendy, but she never kicks it to me.

2 Match the questions with the correct answers.

1. Do you like football?
2. Do you like computer classes?
3. Do you like Bill?
4. Does Tom like you?
5. Does your teacher like you and your classmates?

a. Yes, I like them.
b. Yes, she likes us.
c. Yes, I like it.
d. Yes, I like him.
e. No, he doesn't like me.

3 Complete the sentences with subject and object pronouns.

1. My favorite subject in school is PE. __I__ really like __it__.
2. Bob really doesn't like civics and geography. _____ really doesn't like _____.
3. Mary and Inez love Harry Styles. _____ love _____.
4. Jim hates pop music. _____ hates _____.
5. Jennifer and I hate doing homework. _____ hate _____.

4 Circle the correct words.

1. I like **play / playing** the guitar. I'm really good at **play / playing / it**.
2. He can **speak / speaking** Japanese really well! He loves **studies it / studying it**.
3. We **do / doing** homework after dinner. We like **do / doing** it together.
4. She doesn't **like / mind** her ICT class because she's good at **work / working / it** on computers.
5. Hector hates **dance / dancing** when his friends watch him. He **dances / dancing** when he is at home.

5 Use the -ing form of the verbs to write sentences that express opinion.

Verbs	Opinions
dance	love
~~do~~	like
eat	don't mind
play	don't like
sing	hate
study	
watch	

1. _I love doing karate._
2. _____
3. _____
4. _____
5. _____
6. _____
7. _____

CONVERSATION — What do you want?

1 Put the words in the correct order to make sentences to complete the conversation.

A: go / May / library, / please / I / to / the / ?
May I go to the library, please?

B: for / No. / time / is / It / geography / .
_____

A: But / left / my / geography / in the library / book / I / .
_____

B: can / share / You / a / with / book / Diane / .
_____

A: get / May / I / it / lunch / during / ?
_____

B: No / Sure. / problem / .
_____

2 Complete the sentences.

| But | can | ~~may~~ | sorry | Sure | Thanks |

Justin: Mr. Mitchell, ¹___*may*___ I stay after class for help with math today?

Mr. Mitchell: I'm ²_____, Justin, but I have to go somewhere after school today.

Justin: ³_____ we have a math test tomorrow.

Mr. Mitchell: Haley, ⁴_____ you help Justin after school with math?

Haley: ⁵_____, no problem, Mr. Mitchell.

Mr. Mitchell: ⁶_____, Haley.

34 | Unit 5

READING TO WRITE

1 Put the steps for an email request in order.

_____ Say thank you.

_____ Ask for permission to do something.

__1__ Introduce yourself.

_____ State the problem.

2 Write the email in the correct order. Then label the parts of the email with the words and phrases.

```
To:      
From:    lmichaels@clstudent.cup.org
Subject: 
```

Dear Mr. Sanchez,

Ask for permission.   Closing   Greeting   Introduce yourself.
Say thank you.   State the problem.   Subject line

Dear Mr. Sanchez, ____Greeting____

sanchezt@clmiddleschool.cup.org

I'm a student in your math class. _____

Thank you for considering this. _____

May I stay after school a couple of days for extra help? _____

If you can help me, please let me know what days you can stay.

I try to do my homework, but many times I don't understand it. _____

Math is very hard for me. _____

Best regards, _____

Lee _____

Help with homework _____

I'm Lee Michaels. _____

Unit 5 | 35

Anuj's FIRST DAY

Unit 1 Video 1.1

BEFORE YOU WATCH

1 **Look at the picture from the video. Circle the correct words.**

1. This **is** / **are** a school in India.
2. The boys **is** / **are** students.
3. The students **is** / **are** in class.
4. The teacher **is** / **are** a man.

WHILE YOU WATCH

2 **Watch the video. Are the sentences true (T) or false (F)? Correct the false sentences.**

1. _____ Anuj is 12 years old. _____
2. _____ Anuj eats breakfast with his teacher. _____
3. _____ The school is all girls. _____
4. _____ The students study English. _____
5. _____ The students live at the school. _____

3 **Watch the video again. When do these things happen? Write numbers 1 to 5.**

_____ go to history class

_____ eat breakfast

_____ play games

_____ go to English class

_____ walk in the mountains

AFTER YOU WATCH

4 **Work with a partner. Complete the chart about you and your school.**

Your name	Your age	Your school's name	Your teacher's name
Peter	12	Harris School	Mr. Black

My name is Peter. I am 12 years old. I go to Harris School. My teacher's name is Mr. Black.

Jin Yang: A GYMNAST

Unit 1 Video 1.3

BEFORE YOU WATCH

1 Look at the pictures from the video. Circle the correct words.

1. This girl is a great **gymnast / gymnastics**.

2. The girls in this **gymnast / gymnastics** class are 10 years old.

WHILE YOU WATCH

2 Watch the video. Are the sentences true (*T*) or false (*F*)? Correct the false sentences.

1. _____ Jin Yang lives with her father.   _____

2. _____ Gymnastics practice is every day.   _____

3. _____ Jin Yang sees her mother.   _____

4. _____ Jin Yang runs in the hallway.   _____

5. _____ Jin Yang loves the park.   _____

3 Watch the video again. Match the sentences with the correct words.

1. Jin Yang is 12 _____ old.   a. father

2. Her class is all _____.   b. difficult

3. Her teacher is a _____.   c. man

4. Jin Yang and her _____ are at the park.   d. years

5. The gymnastics class is very _____.   e. girls

AFTER YOU WATCH

4 Discuss: What club or sport do you like? Why?

> I like science. It's very interesting. I am in a science club at school.

> I like painting. I go to an art class every day after school.

Unit 1 | 73

The YELLOW FERRARI

Unit 2 Video 2.1

BEFORE YOU WATCH

1 Look at the pictures. Circle the correct words.

1. This is Maria. She is **12 / 17 / 30** years old.

2. This is her **car / bike / boat**.

3. Maria's car is really **fast / slow / old**.

4. This is Maria's **brother / family / friend**.

WHILE YOU WATCH

2 Watch the video. Are the sentences true (*T*) or false (*F*)? Correct the false sentences.

1. _____ Maria lives in Spain.   _____

2. _____ Maria's car is blue.   _____

3. _____ Maria's favorite car is the Ferrari. _____

4. _____ Maria is a student.   _____

5. _____ Maria is first in the race.   _____

3 Complete the sentences with the correct words.

1. Ferraris are _____ cars.

2. _____ is a city in Italy.

3. Maria's teacher is a _____ .

4. Maria has an _____ race.

5. Maria's _____ goes to the race.

Italian
important
man
Rome
family

AFTER YOU WATCH

4 Work with a partner.

1. Work with a partner. Say a country. Your partner names a car from that country. Take turns.

   (Japan.)   (Toyota.)

2. Discuss: What is your favorite car?

   (My favorite car is a Ford.)

74 | Unit 2

Young SCIENTISTS

Unit 2 Video 2.3

BEFORE YOU WATCH

1 Look at the pictures. Complete the sentences with the correct words.

golf   laptop   scientists

1. I write my papers on my _____.
2. He is playing _____.
3. These _____ study chemistry.

WHILE YOU WATCH

2 Watch the video. Circle the correct answers.

1. The students are all from _____.
   a. Washington D.C.   b. Hawaii   c. the United States
2. They all love _____.
   a. golf   b. science   c. music
3. Jack's favorite sport is _____.
   a. tennis   b. soccer   c. golf
4. Michael's favorite thing is a red _____.
   a. plane   b. train   c. phone
5. Melissa is a student and a _____.
   a. musician   b. teacher   c. tennis player

3 Watch the video again. Match the people with the places.

Who	Place
1. Jack _____	a. Missouri
2. Michael _____	b. Hawaii
3. Avni _____	c. Illinois
4. Melissa _____	d. Pennsylvania

AFTER YOU WATCH

4 Work with a partner. Complete the chart. Talk about your favorite things.

My favorite . . .

Country	City	Sport	Singer
Spain	Madrid	soccer	Katy Perry

My favorite country is Spain. My favorite city is Madrid. I love soccer. I really like Katy Perry!

Robot FIGHTERS

Unit 3 Video 3.1

BEFORE YOU WATCH

1 Write the correct words next to the pictures from the video.

daughter   father   mother   prizes   robot

1. _____

2. _____

3. _____

4. _____

5. _____

WHILE YOU WATCH

2 Watch the video. Check (✓) the sentences you hear.

1. This is my uncle and his family. _____

2. This is my sister. _____

3. Hiroshi makes the prizes. _____

4. My aunt's robot is in the competition, too. _____

5. Arina gets a prize. _____

6. She's really tall! _____

3 Watch the video again. Are the sentences true (T) or false (F)? Correct the false sentences.

1. _____ The family lives in London. _____

2. _____ Tokyo is in China. _____

3. _____ The girl is 11 years old. _____

4. _____ The girl loves video games. _____

5. _____ The mother's robot has long, white hair. _____

6. _____ The mother and the daughter get a prize. _____

AFTER YOU WATCH

4 Work in small groups. Describe your family. What are their names? What do they like doing?

> My father's name is David. He likes playing golf.
> My mother's name is Mona. She likes reading.

My SIBERIAN FAMILY

Unit 3 Video 3.3

BEFORE YOU WATCH

1 Match the words with the pictures from the video.

Siberia   reindeer   Khanty people

1. _____   2. _____   3. _____

2 Now complete the sentences with the words from the video.

_____ is in the north of Russia. My grandparents are _____. They have a lot of _____.

WHILE YOU WATCH

3 Watch the video. When do you see these things? Write numbers 1 to 5.

_____ the boy and his father

_____ the grandparents

_____ the reindeer

_____ the snowmobile

_____ the town

4 Watch the video again. Circle the correct answers.

1. Siberia is in _____.
   a. Norway   b. Russia   c. China
2. The grandparents have about _____ reindeer.
   a. 5   b. 15   c. 50
3. The boy's town is very _____.
   a. small   b. short   c. big
4. The town has _____ store(s).
   a. one   b. two   c. three
5. The boy and his father _____ at the grandparents' house.
   a. work   b. play   c. work and play

AFTER YOU WATCH

5 Work with a partner. Who is your favorite family member? Where does he or she live? Who does he or she live with?

> My favorite relative is my Aunt Hilda. She lives in Mexico City. She lives with my Uncle Carlos.

Unit 3 | 77

Ali's DAY

Unit 4 Video 4.1

BEFORE YOU WATCH

1 Match the sentences with the pictures from the video.

a.   b.   c.

1. Cairo is a very big city in Egypt. _____
2. This is Ali at work. He makes bread in the mornings. _____
3. Ali takes bread to people on his bike. _____

WHILE YOU WATCH

2 Watch the video. Complete the sentences with the correct number.

| 5 | 6 | 7 | 15 | 17 |

1. Ali is _____ years old.
2. He works _____ hours a day.
3. He works _____ days a week.
4. He gets up at _____ o'clock every morning.
5. He goes to work at _____ o'clock.

3 Watch the video again. Circle the correct answers.

1. Where does Ali live?
    a. Istanbul   b. Cairo   c. Paris
2. What does he do during the day?
    a. takes flowers to people   b. plays tennis   c. makes bread
3. When does Ali take things to people?
    a. in the evening   b. in the morning and the afternoon   c. at midnight
4. Who does Ali eat with?
    a. his friends from work   b. his friends from school   c. his family

AFTER YOU WATCH

4 Work with a partner. Who in your family works? Say four things they do every day. When do they do them? Take turns.

> My mother works. She always gets up at 6:00. She eats breakfast at 7:00. She comes home at 5:00. She usually watches TV at night.

La QUINCEAÑERA

Unit 4 Video 4.3

BEFORE YOU WATCH

1 Match the words with the correct pictures.

dance   dress   ring   rose

1. _____   2. _____   3. _____   4. _____

WHILE YOU WATCH

2 Watch the video. Are the sentences true (*T*) or false (*F*)? Correct the false sentences.

1. _____ Monterrey is a big city in Mexico. _____

2. _____ Priscilla is at school with her sister. _____

3. _____ School finishes at three o'clock. _____

4. _____ Priscilla plays water polo after school on Mondays and Thursdays. _____

5. _____ Priscilla is 16 today. _____

3 Watch the video again. Complete the sentences.

1. Girls always wear a special _____ to their party.

2. Parents give a special _____ to their daughter at the party.

3. Priscilla first dance is with her _____.

4. Priscilla father, brother, and grandfather give her a _____.

5. At the end of the party, Priscilla _____ with her friends.

AFTER YOU WATCH

4 Work in small groups. Discuss: How do you celebrate your birthday?

> I have a party on my birthday. My friends come to the party. We play games and we eat cake and ice cream.

Kung Fu SCHOOL

Unit 5 Video 5.1

BEFORE YOU WATCH

1 Match the words with the correct pictures.

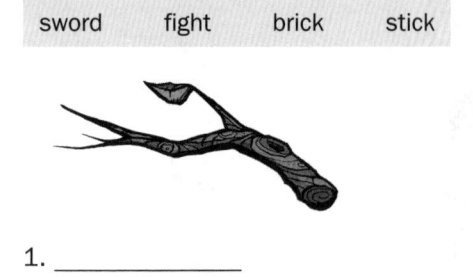

sword   fight   brick   stick

1. _____

2. _____

3. _____

4. _____

WHILE YOU WATCH

2 Watch the video. Complete the sentences with the correct adjectives.

beautiful   famous   old   quiet

Song Shan is a very ¹_____ town in the mountains. It's ²_____ and ³_____. It also has a ⁴_____ traditional kung fu school.

3 Watch the video again. Answer the questions.

1. Where is Song Shan? _____

2. Who is Master Li Yu? _____

3. What do the students do each morning? _____

4. What do the students fight with? _____

5. How many boys study at the school? _____

6. What time do they eat lunch? _____

7. Students at the school learn to fight. What else do they learn? _____

AFTER YOU WATCH

4 Work with a partner. What sports do the students at your school play? Make a list. What are your two favorites?

> Students at my school play basketball, soccer, baseball, and tennis. My favorites are basketball and baseball.

Tobilay's SCHOOL DAY

Unit 5 Video 5.3

BEFORE YOU WATCH

1. Look at the picture from the video. Complete the sentences with the correct words.

   netball   PE   South Africa

   These students live in _____. They're in a _____ class. The name of this sport is _____. It's similar to basketball.

WHILE YOU WATCH

2. Watch the video. Complete the sentences with the numbers.

   5   8   14   300

   1. Tobilay is _____ years old.
   2. School starts at _____ o'clock.
   3. The national song of South Africa has words from _____ languages in it.
   4. The school makes lunch for _____ children.

3. Watch the video again. Number the events in the order that they happen from 1 to 6.

   _____ Tobilay walks to school.
   _____ The children learn traditional South African songs and dances.
   _____ Tobilay plays netball with her classmates.
   _____ Tobilay has class.
   _____ The students eat lunch.
   _____ Tobilay and the other students sing the national song.

AFTER YOU WATCH

4. Write about your day at school. What do you like doing? What don't you like doing? How is your day different from Tobilay's day?

   School starts at 8:00 o'clock. I usually have English class first . . .

Unit 5 | 81

This page intentionally left blank.

Irregular verbs

Base Verb	Simple Past
be	was, were
become	became
break	broke
build	built
buy	bought
can	could
choose	chose
come	came
do	did
draw	drew
drink	drank
drive	drove
eat	ate
fall	fell
feel	felt
find	found
fly	flew
get	got
give	gave
go	went
hang	hung
have	had
hear	heard
hold	held

Base Verb	Simple Past
know	knew
leave	left
lose	lost
make	made
meet	met
pay	paid
read	read
ride	rode
run	ran
say	said
see	saw
sell	sold
send	sent
sit	sat
sleep	slept
speak	spoke
spend	spent
swim	swam
take	took
teach	taught
think	thought
understand	understood
wear	wore
win	won

Credits

The publishers are grateful to the following for permission to reproduce copyright photographs and material:

Cover: ©John Hyde/Alamy; Back Cover (B/G): Shutterstock Images/photosoft; p. 2-3 (B/R) Alamy/© Blend Images; p. 4 (L) Shutterstock Images/Exactostock; p. 4 (T) Shutterstock Images/pukach; p. 4 (CR) © Radius Images / Alamy; p. 4 (c) Shutterstock Images/Sabphoto; p. 4 (TR) Shutterstock Images/Alan Poulson Photography; p. 5 (CR) Shutterstock Images/Armin Staudt; p. 6 (B/G) Shutterstock Images/FredS; p. 6 (TC) Shutterstock Images/sixninepixels; p. 6 (TR) Shutterstock Images/Dundanim; p. 6 (CR) Shutterstock Images/IngridHS; p. 6 (CL) Shutterstock Images/Pinkcandy; p. 6 (CL) Shutterstock Images/Tom Saga; p. 6 (BL) Alamy/© Radius Images; p. 6 (BC) Shutterstock Images/xavier gallego morell; p. 6 (BL) Shutterstock Images/hxdbzxy; p. 6 (TL) Shutterstock Images/Tyler Olson; p. 7 (TR) Shutterstock Images/Pressmaster; p. 8 (BL) Shutterstock Images/Pressmaster; p. 8 (TL) Shutterstock Images/KonstantinChristian; p. 8 (BC) Shutterstock Images/Sittipong; p. 8 (BCR) Shutterstock Images/Ingvar Bjork; p. 8 (BCL) Shutterstock Images/Phant; p. 10 (B/G) Shutterstock Images/pisaphotography; p. 10 (TCL) Superstock/Ambient Images Inc. ; p. 10 (TL) Alamy/© TNT Magazine; p. 10 (B/G) Shutterstock Images/Songquan Deng; p. 10 (TR) Shutterstock Images/yanugkelid; p. 10 (TL) Shutterstock Images/igor.stevanovic; 10 (TCL) Alamy/© David Grossman; p. 11 (CL) Shutterstock Images/zirconicusso; p. 11 (TC) Shutterstock Images/ribeiroantonio; p. 11 (TL) Shutterstock Images/edel; p. 11 (BC) Shutterstock Images/ID1974; p. 12-13 (B/G) Shutterstock Images/Omegafoto; p. 12 (C) Shutterstock Images/Joana Lopes; p. 12 (inset) Image provided by the SeaWiFS Project; NASA/Goddard Space Flight Center; and ORBIMAGE; p. 13 (9) Shutterstock Images/Brian A Jackson; p. 13 (1): iStockphoto/AnthonyRosenberg; p. 13 (4): ©Richard Sharrocks / Alamy; p. 13 (6): ©graficart.net / Alamy; p. 13 (10): ©Andres Rodriguez / Alamy; p. 13 (11): ©Lusoimages - Technology / Alamy; p. 13 (12): ©music Alan King / Alamy; p. 13 (2) Shutterstock Images/artjazz; p. 13 (5R) LES BREAULT/©Alamy; p. 13 (5) Alamy/© LES BREAULT ; p. 13 (5) Alamy/©FILM STILLS; p. 13 (7) Shuttertstock Images/Denys Prykhodov; p. 13 (8) Alamy/©Nikreates; p. 14 (L): ©DEAN LEWINS/epa/Corbis; p. 14 (R): ©DANIEL MUNOZ/Reuters/Corbis; p. 16 (TL) Alamy/©Paul Paddison ; p. 17 (CR) Alamy/©RubberBall; p. 18 (BC) Shutterstock Images/Dan Thornberg; p. 18 (TL) Shutterstock Images/dotshock; p. 18 (BR) Shutterstock Images/Lightspring; p. 18 (BL) Shutterstock Images/Michael Rosskothen; p. 19 (TR) Shutterstock Images/pedalist; p. 20 (CR) Shutterstock Images/iQoncept; p. 20 (TR) Shutterstock Images/art-Tayga; p. 20 (CR) Shutterstock Images/Globe Turner; p. 20 (BC) Shutterstock Images/Manczurov; p. 20 (TR) Shutterstock Images/Stephen Firmender; p. 21 (TL) Shutterstock Images/cristovao; p. 21 (BL) Shutterstock Images/cristovao; p. 21 (C) Alamy/©David Young-Wolff; p. 22-23 (B/G) Shutterstock Images/Cora Mueller; p. 23 (L): ©Blend Images / Alamy; p. 23 (CL): Stock Connection / SuperStock; p. 23 (BL): Shutterstock/Angela Hawkey; p. 23 (BCL): Gareth Boden; p.23 (BC): ©imagebroker / Alamy; p. 23 (TR): Shutterstock/Jacek Chabraszewski; p. 23 (CR) Shutterstock Images/aastock; p. 23 (TCR) Shutterstock Images/Stuart Monk; p. 23 (BC) Alamy/©moodboard ; p. 23 (BCR) Shutterstock Images/Monkey Business Images; p. 23 (CR) Shutterstock Images/aastock; p. 23 (TCL) Shutterstock Images/photobank.ch; p. 23 (TCR) Shutterstock Images/racorn; p. 24 (B/G) Shutterstock Images/ffolas ; p. 24 (T): Photo Kevin Farmer / APN; p. 24 (BL): Photo Kevin Farmer / APN; p. 26 (B/G) © Kathleen Smith / Alamy; p. 26 (B/G) Alamy/©Kathleen Smith; p. 27 (R) Shutterstock Images/CREATISTA; p. 28 (BL) Shutterstock Images/Popartic; p. 28 (TL) Alamy/©PhotoAlto; p. 28 (CT): Shutterstock/CREATISTA; p. 28 (CB): Shutterstock/Photosindiacom, LLC; p. 28 (B): ©Young-Wolff Photography / Alamy; p. 29 (T): ©RubberBall / Alamy; p. 30 (TR): ©India Picture/Corbis; p. 30 (TL): Shutterstock/v.s.anandhakrishna; p. 30 (B/G) Shutterstock Images/Shyamalamuralinath; p. 31 (3) Shutterstock Images/milezaway; p. 31 (1) Shutterstock Images/Monkey Business Images; p. 31 (2) Shutterstock Images/Blend Images; p. 31 (5) Shutterstock Images/Ollyy; p. 31 (4) Shutterstock Images/Gina Smith; p. 31 (3) Alamy/©Stock Connection Distribution; p. 32-33 (c) © Mark A. Johnson/Corbis; p. 33 (i) Shutterstock Images/johnfoto18; p. 33 (b) Shutterstock Images/Kamira; p. 33 (a) Shutterstock Images/Maridav; p. 33 (BL) Superstock/Blend Images; p. 33 (j) Alamy/©Megapress; p. 33 (g) Alamy/©whiteboxmedia limited ; p. 33 (f) Shutterstock Images/philippou; p. 33 (e) Shutterstock Images/Africa Studio; p. 33 (d) Shutterstock Images/RoJo Images; p. 33 (c) Alamy/©Image Source; p. 34 (T) Shutterstock Images/Tracy Whiteside; p. 34 (BL) Alamy/©Megapress; p. 34 (C) Shutterstock Images/Tracy Whiteside; p. 34 (TL) Shutterstock Images/Olyina; p. 35 (CL) Shutterstock Images/Jorg Hackemann; p. 36 (g) Shutterstock Images/Anna Jurkovska; p. 36 (h) Shutterstock Images/Andrey Yurlov; p. 36 (f) Shutterstock Images/Zhukov Oleg; 36 (e) Shutterstock Images/Mike Flippo; p. 36 (d) Shutterstock Images/Be Good; p. 36 (c) Shutterstock Images/Rob Marmion; p. 36 (b) Shutterstock Images/Photosani; p. 36 (a) Shutterstock Images/dean bertoncelj; p. 36 (TL) Corbis/©68/Ocean; p. 37 (TR) Shutterstock Images/nakamasa; p. 38 (CL) Shutterstock Images/Jeka; p. 38 (BC) Shutterstock Images/Maria Maarbes; p. 39 (TL) Shutterstock Images/Max Topchii; p. 40 (TR) Shutterstock Images/Visun Khankasem; p. 40 (BC) Alamy/©epa european pressphoto agency b.v. ; p. 40 (CR) Superstock/age fotostock; p. 40 (CR) Alamy/©Richard Levine; p. 40 (B/G) Shutterstock Images/CHAINFOTO24; p. 42-43 (C) Corbis/©Hero Images; p. 43 (10) Shutterstock Images/Monkey Business Images; p. 43 (9) Shutterstock Images/hxdbzxy; p. 43 (8) Alamy/©B. Leighty/Photri Image; p. 43 (7) Alamy/©Art Directors & TRIP ; p. 43 (6) Shutterstock Images/Gina Smith; p. 43 (5) Alamy/©Blend Images ; p. 43 (4) Alamy/©apply pictures; p. 43 (3) Shutterstock Images/michaeljung; p. 43 (2) Alamy/©Janine Wiedel Photolibrary; p. 44 (BG): ©Chen Xiaodong/Xinhua Press/Corbis; p. 44 (C): ©F. Jack Jackson / Alamy; p. 45 (TR) Shutterstock Images/mekCar; p. 46 (TC) Alamy/©Jack Carey; p. 47 Alamy/©China Images ; p. 48 Shutterstock Images/BrianWancho; p. 49 Alamy/©Radius Images; p. 50 (B/G) Shutterstock Images/art_of_sun; p. 50 (B/G) Alamy/©Christina Kennedy; p. 50 (c) Alamy/©B.O'Kane; p. 50 (a) Alamy/©Stock Connection Blue; p. 50 (b) Alamy/©Blend Images; p. 51 (5) Shutterstock Images/Dancestrokes; p. 51 (6) Shutterstock Images/Pablo Hidalgo; p. 51 (2) Shutterstock Images/mrHanson; p. 51 (4) Shutterstock Images/Olinchuk; p. 51 (1) Alamy/©Michael Neelon; p. 52 (B/G): Stuart Westmorland/Image Source/Corbis; p. 54 Shutterstock Images/Gyorgy Barna ; p. 54-55 (B/G) Shutterstock Images/photka; p. 55 (12) Shutterstock Images/jantarus; p. 55 (11) Shutterstock Images/Olga Popova; p. 55 (10) Shutterstock Images/VladaKela; p. 55 (17) Shutterstock Images/fototip; p. 55 (13) Shutterstock Images/Gregory Gerber; p. 55 (14) Shutterstock Images/indigolotos; p. 55 (16) Shutterstock Images/Alex Studio; p. 55 (17) Shutterstock Images/Hurst Photo; p. 55 (15) Shutterstock Images/Naufal MQ; p. 55 (2) Shutterstock Images/KIM NGUYEN; p. 55 (9) Shutterstock Images/KIM NGUYEN; p. 55 (7) Shutterstock Images/Maks Narodenko; p. 55 (1) Shutterstock Images/Nagritsamon Ruksujjar; 55 (3) Shutterstock Images/Alex Studio; p. 55 (4) Shutterstock Images/EM Arts; p. 55 (5) Shutterstock Images/hannadarzy; 55 (6) Shutterstock Images/Michal Nowosielski; p. 55 (8) Shutterstock Images/Yakov Oskanov; p. 56 (TR): ©Manzo Niikura/amanaimages/Corbis; p. 56 (CL): ©MIXA / Alamy; p. 56 (CR): ©MIXA / Alamy; p. 56 (B/G) Shutterstock Images/JOAT; p. 56 (C) Shutterstock Images/Nataliya Arzamasova; p. 58 (j) Shutterstock Images/amphaiwan; p. 58 (c) Alamy/©amana images inc.. p. 58 (TL) Shutterstock Images/Diana Taliun; p. 58 (a) Alamy/©imageBROKER ; p. 58 (b) Shutterstock Images/Shebeko; p. 58 (e) Shutterstock Images/dotshock; p. 58 (k) Alamy/©whiteboxmedia limited ; p. 58 (i) Shutterstock Images/Active branding; p. 58 (f) Alamy/©Handmade Pictures ; p. 58 (h) Shutterstock Images/Hurst Photo; p. 59 (BR) Shutterstock Images/Sally Scott; p. 60 (TL) Alamy/©Image Source; p. 60 (BL) Shutterstock Images/Grounder; p. 60 (BL) Shutterstock Images/mahmuttibet; p. 61 (TR) Shutterstock Images/Petr Jilek; p. 62 (TR) courtesy of Dominic Lau/Don Chow Tacos; p. 62 (CL) courtesy of Dominic Lau/Don Chow Tacos; p. 62 (CR) courtesty of Virginia Ginsburg; p. 62 (B/G) Shutterstock Images/Annareichel; p. 62 (B/G) Shutterstock Images/giftzyx; p. 64-65 (B/G): Shutterstock/Sylvie Bouchard; p. 66 (TL): Fotosearch / SuperStock; p. 66 (CL): ©tbkmedia.de / Alamy; p. 66 (BL): ©Joe McDonald/Corbis; p. 66 (TR): Thomas Marent/Minden Pictures/FLPA; p. 66: (a) Shutterstock Images/Kletr; p. 66: (b) Shutterstock Images/Piotr Krzeslak; p. 66: (f) Glow Images/Jevgenija Pigozne/ImageBROKER; p. 66: (h) Shutterstock Images/Michiel de Wit; p. 67 (TR): Frans Lanting/FLPA; p. 67: (B/G) Shutterstock Images/Aleksandr Bryliaev; p. 68: (T) Alamy/©frans lemmens; p. 68: (1) Shutterstock Images/Jeff Dalton; p. 68: (2) Shutterstock Images/Shane Myers Photography; p. 68: (3) Alamy/©Juniors Bildarchiv GmbH; p. 68: (4) SuperStock/Biosphoto; p. 68: (5) SuperStock/NHPA; p.68: (6) Masterfile/Minden Pictures; p. 68: (7) SuperStock/©Frank Sommariva/image/imagebroker.net; p. 69 (TR): ©i love images / women's lifestyle / Alamy; p. 70 (B/G) Shutterstock Images/Abigail210986; p. 70: (TL) Alamy/©Kumar Sriskandan; p.70: (TR) Shutterstock Images/stevemart; p. 70: (BL) Shutterstock Images/ntstudio; p. 71 (TR): ©Arletta Cwalina / Alamy; p. 72: (TL) Shutterstock Images/mariait; p. 72 (TR): Getty Images/Wayne R Bilenduke; p. 72 (BC); imagebroker.net / SuperStock; p. 74-75: (B/G) Getty Images/Martin Puddy; p. 75 (a): ©OJO Images Ltd / Alamy; p. 75 (b): ©Radius Images / Alamy; p. 75 (c): ©Andrew Fox / Alamy; p. 75 (d): ©Randy Faris/Corbis; p. 75 (f): Tony Garcia / SuperStock; p. 75 (g): ©Bubbles Photolibrary / Alamy; p. 75: (e) SuperStock/©Flirt; p. 75: (h) Alamy/©El Chapulin; p. 75: (i) SuperStock/©Allindiaimages; p. 75: (j) Masterfile/andresr/Crestock; p. 76 (T): ©Ammit / Alamy; p. 76 (B): Tony Waltham/Robert Harding; p. 76 (CL): ©Robert Harding Picture Library Ltd / Alamy; p. 76 (CL): Peter Barritt / Robert Harding Picture Library / SuperStock; p. 77: (CR) Media Bakery/Matz Sjöberg; p. 78: (T) Alamy/© D. Hurst; p. 78: (a) Alamy/©Peter Horree; p. 78: (b) Alamy/©Caro; p. 78: (c) Shutterstock Images/Andrey Khrolenok; p. 78: (d) Alamy/©LOOK Die Bildagentur der Fotografen GmbH; p. 78: (e) Shutterstock Images/Dabarti CGI; p. 78: (f) Alamy/©Richard Levine; p. 78: (g) Alamy/©Don Klumpp; p. 78: (h) Shutterstock Images/guroldinneden; p. 79: (BR) Alamy/©Kumar Sriskandan; p. 80: (T) Masterfile/David Zimmerman; p. 80: (2) Shutterstock Images/CristinaMuraca; p. 80: (3) Shutterstock Images/Oleksiy Mark; p. 80: (BL) Shutterstock Images/Leanne Vorrias; p. 81: (TR) Shutterstock Images/Alberto Loyo; p. 82: (B/G) Shutterstock Images/gyn9037; p. 82: (1) age fotostock/© Fumio; p. 82 (CT): ©DBURKE / Alamy; p. 82 (CL): ©Tetra Images / Alamy; p. 82 (CB): ©dbimages / Alamy; p. 82 (CB): ©UrbanEye / Alamy; p. 84-85 (B/G): ©Aurora Photos / Alamy; p. 85: (1) Shutterstock Images/StacieStauffSmith Photos; p. 85 (2): Shutterstock/gorillaimages; p. 85 (3): Shutterstock/Tom Gowanlock; p. 85 (5): ©Aflo Foto Agency / Alamy; p. 85 (7): ©Shaun Wilkinson / Alamy; p. 85 (10): Getty Images/Happy to share the beauty I see in my travels; p. 85 (11): Thinkstock; p. 85: (4) Shutterstock Images/pio3; p. 85: (6) Alamy/©Andres Rodriguez; p. 85: (8) Shutterstock Images/EcoPrint; p. 85: (9) Shutterstock Images/Andrey_Popov; p. 86 (TL): ©Bernard Bisson/Sygma/Corbis; p. 87: (TR) SuperStock/©Exactostock; p. 88: (T) Shutterstock Images/Marco Prati; p. 88: (a) Shutterstock Images/mimon!; p. 88: (b) Shutterstock Images/Alexander Kalina; p. 88: (c) Shutterstock Images/Neveshkin Nikolay; p. 88: (d) Shutterstock Images/Vlue; p. 88: (e) Shutterstock Images/Elnur; p. 88: (f) Shutterstock Images/Karkas; p. 88: (g) Alamy/©D. Hurst; p. 88: (h) Shutterstock Images/Elnur; p. 88: (i) Shutterstock Images/Petar Djordjevic; p. 88: (j) Shutterstock Images/Vlue; p. 88: (k) Shutterstock Images/In Green; p. 88: (L) Shutterstock Images/Karkas; p. 89: (CR) Shutterstock Images/Maxim Blinkov; p. 90: (T) Shutterstock Images/Pistryy Valeriy; p. 90: (2) Shutterstock Images/Pavel L Photo and Video; p. 90: (3) Shutterstock Images/pryzmat; p. 90: (4) Alamy/©Extreme Sports Photo; p. 91: (T) Alamy/©epa european pressphoto agency b.v.; p. 92: (bkgd t) Alamy/©dbimages; p. 92: (TR) Shutterstock Images/James Steidl; p. 94-95 (B/G): Panos/Fredrik Naumann; p. 95: (8) Alamy/©PhotoStock-Israel; p. 96: (a) Alamy/©Westend61 GmbH; p. 95 (1): ©Angie Sharp / Alamy; p. 95 (2): PETER SKINNER/SCIENCE PHOTO LIBRARY; p. 95 (3): ©Juniors Bildarchiv GmbH / Alamy; p. 95 (4): London News Pictures/Rex Features; p. 95 (5): ©Fredrick Kippe / Alamy; p. 95 (6): ©Design Pics Inc. / Alamy; p. 95 (7): ©Radius Images/Corbis; p. 95 (B): ©Gay Bumgarner / Alamy; p. 96: (b) Alamy/©Gary Dublanko; p. 96: (c) Alamy/©i travel; p. 97: (T) Shutterstock Images/monticello; p. 98: (T) Alamy/©Robert Fried; p. 98: (2) Shutterstock Images/Vlada Z; p. 98 (6): ©travelbild.com / Alamy; p. 98: (3) Shutterstock Images/David Krijgsman; p. 98: (4) Shutterstock Images/Matt Tilghman; p. 98: (5) Shutterstock Images/Meg007; p. 98: (BL) Shutterstock Images/Steve Whiston; p. 99: (TR) Shutterstock Images/EllenSmile; p. 99: (BR) Shutterstock Images/Arsgera; p. 100: (TL) SuperStock/©Cusp; p. 100: (BL) Shutterstock Images/Chaikovskiy Igor; p. 101: (TR) Newscom/Bettina Strenske imageBROKER; p. 102: (B/G) Shutterstock Images/Krishna.Wu; p. 102: (TL) Shutterstock Images/Marques; p. 102 (TL): ©Egmont Strigl / Alamy; p. 102 (CL): Shutterstock/B Calkins; p. 102 (BL): ©Richard Hamilton Smith/CORBIS; p.102 (TR): Bill Coster/FLPA; p. 102 (CR): ©Oleksiy Maksymenko/All Canada Photos/Corbis; p. 102 (CR): ©Free Agents Limited/CORBIS; p. 102 (BR): ©CBW / Alamy; p. 104-105: (B/G) SuperStock/©Dave Fleetham/Pacific Stock - Design Pics; p. 117 (TC) Shutterstock Images/Mike Peters; p. 117 (CR) Shutterstock Images/Edith60; p. 117 (CL) Shutterstock Images/Dominique de La Croix; p. 119: (1) Alamy/©Joshua Dale Rablin; p. 119: (2) Shutterstock Images/Stayer; p. 119: (3) Shutterstock Images/Mr. SUTTIPON YAKHAM; p. 119: (4) Shutterstock Images/Audrey Snider-Bell; p. 120: (TR) Alamy/©Peter Barritt; p. 120: (CR) Shutterstock Images/clivewa

The publishers are grateful to the following illustrators:

David Belmonte (Beehive Illustration) p. 26, 27
Anni Betts pp. 52, 53, 104, 105
Nigel Dobbyn (Beehive Illustration) p. 119
Ian Escott (Beehive Illustration) p. 73
Q2A Media Services, Inc. p. 3, 16, 34, 46, 59, 70, 78, 83, 117, 118
Jose Rubio p. 57, 63
Sean Tiffany p. 4, 8, 44, 67, 69.

All video stills by kind permission of:

Discovery Communications, LLC 2015: p. 2 (1,3), 8, 10, 12 (1, 3, 4), 15, 20, 21, 22 (1, 3, 4), 25, 30, 32 (1, 3, 4, 35, 38, 40, 41, 42 (1, 3), 45, 51, 54 (1, 3, 4), 57, 62, 63, 64 (1, 3, 4), 67, 72, 73, 74 (1, 3, 4), 77, 82, 84 (1, 3), 87, 92, 94 (1, 3, 4), 97, 103. 116, 117, 118, 119, 120
Cambridge University Press: p. 2 (2), 8, 12 (2), 18, 22 (2), 28, 32 (2), 42 (2), 48, 54 (2), 60, 64 (2), 70, 74 (2), 80, 84 (2), 90, 94 (2), 100

Credits

Photo Credits:

Cover: ©John Hyde/Alamy; Back Cover (B/G): Shutterstock Images/photosoft; p. 10 (TL): REX/Startraks Photo; p. 10 (TR): Tony Gonzalez/Everett Collection/Alamy; p. 10 (CL): Featureflash/Shutterstock; p. 10 (CR): Dfree/Shutterstock; p. 10 (BL): REX/Startraks Photo; p 10 (BR): Everett Collection/Shutterstock; p. 11 (TL): Image Source/SuperStock; p. 11 (BR): Datacraft - Sozaijiten/Alamy; p. 17 (TL): ©Richard Sharrocks / Alamy; p. 17 (TR): iStockphoto/AnthonyRosenberg; p. 17 (CL): ©Art Directors & TRIP / Alamy; p. 17 (CR): ©Caro / Alamy; p. 17 (BL): ©music Alan King / Alamy; p. 17 (BR): ©graficart.net / Alamy; p. 21 (T): Featureflash/Shutterstock; p. 23: Getty/Adrianna Williams/The Image Bank; p. 30 (1): Alamy/Archimage; p. 30 (2): Alamy/Janine Wiedel Photolibrary; p. 30 (3): Alamy/Andrew Fox; p. 30 (4): Alamy/Mike Booth; p. 30 (5): Alamy/Archimage; p. 30 (6): Alamy/redsnapper; p. 30 (7): Alamy/Peter Titmuss; p. 30 (8): Shutterstock/Monkey Business Images; p. 30 (9): Alamy/Janine Wiedel Photolibrary; p. 30 (10): Alamy/VIEW Pictures Ltd.; p. 36 (a): Shutterstock/Larina Natalia; p. 36 (b): Alamy/Richard Levine; p. 36 (c): KIM NGUYEN/Shutterstock; p. 36 (d): Shutterstock/Lasse Kristensen; p. 36 (e): Shutterstock/MaraZe; p. 36 (f): Olga Popova/Shutterstock; p. 36 (g): Alamy/John James; p. 36 (h): Shutterstock/Robyn Mackenzie; p. 36 (i): jantarus/Shutterstock; p. 37 (L): Alamy/Hera Food; p. 37 (R): Shutterstock/foodiepics; p. 40 (L): Shutterstock/zirconicusso; p. 40 (T): Shutterstock/Studiotouch; p. 40 (B): Shutterstock/highviews; p. 45 (1): Alamy/Sarah Peters/imagebroker; p. 45 (2): Getty/ranplett/Vetta; p. 45 (3): Superstock/Science Photo Library; p. 45 (4): Alamy/kpzfoto; p. 45 (5): Shutterstock/andamanec; p. 45 (6): Superstock/Tips Images; p. 45 (TR): Blend Images/Shutterstock; p. 46 (TL): Alamy/©Juniors Bildarchiv GmbH; p. 46 (TCL): Shutterstock Images/Shane Myers Photography; p. 46 (BCL): SuperStock/NHPA; p. 46 (BL): SuperStock/©Frank Sommariva/image/ imagebroker.net; p. 46 (TR): Shutterstock Images/Jeff Dalton; p. 46 (CR): SuperStock/Biosphoto; p. 46 (BR): Masterfile/Minden Pictures; p. 47 (L):Alamy/Dallas and John Heaton/Travel Pictures; p. 47 (C): Alamy/David Cantrille; p. 47 (R): Getty/David Wall Photo/Lonely Planet Images; p. 49 (TR): Vladimir Melnik/Shutterstock; p. 49 (CR): MartinMaritz/Shutterstock; p. 50 (a): fiphoto/Shutterstock; p. 50 (b): Getty/Atlantide S.N.C./age fotostock; p. 50 (c): Alamy/PBimages; p. 50 (d): ValeStock/Shutterstock; p. 50 (e): Alamy/Marc Macdonald; p. 50 (f): Alamy/eye35.pix; p. 50 (g): Alamy/Aardvark; p. 50 (h): Shutterstock/Tischenko Irina; p. 50 (i): Alamy/Stephen Dorey ABIPP; p. 50 (j): Alamy/incamerastock; p. 55 (TR): Rob Marmion/Shutterstock; p. 56 (a): ChameleonsEye/Shutterstock; p. 56 (b): Paul Banton/Shutterstock; p. 56 (c): Ulrich Mueller/Shutterstock; p. 56 (d): Walter Bibikow/Mauritius/SuperStock; p. 56 (e): Glow Images/SuperStock; p. 56 (f): Robert Kneschke/Shutterstock; p. 56 (g): nodff/Shutterstock; p. 56 (h): FloridaStock/Shutterstock; p. 56 (i): Smereka/Shutterstock; p. 56 (j): Franck Boston/Shutterstock; p. 58 (T1): Ipatov/Shutterstock; p. 58 (T2): Getty/technotr/E+; p. 58 (T4): Shutterstock/oliveromg; p. 58 (T5): Shutterstock/Jacek Chabraszewski; p. 58 (T7): tammykayphoto/Shutterstock; p. 58 (T9): Tony Garcia / SuperStock; p. 58 (B2): Shutterstock/Petrenko Andriy; p. 58 (B3): Alamy/PictureNet Corporation; p. 58 (B6): Corbis/Chris Cole/Duomo; p. 58 (B8): Pistryy Valeriy/Shutterstock; p. 58 (B10): Getty/Mike Kemp; p. 58 (B11): Shutterstock/YanLev; p. 63 (T): lev radin/Shutterstock

The publishers are grateful to the following illustrators:

Janet Allinger p. 6, 20, 34, 54, 68; David Belmonte (Beehive Illustration) p. 3, 4, 26, 38, 59, 60, 61; Anni Betts p. 13, 22, 67, 70, 75; Galia Bernstein (NB Illustration) p. 17,19, 51; Alberto de Hoyos p. 53; Nigel Dobbyn (Beehive Illustration) p. 33, 40, 41, 48, 79; Q2A Media Services, Inc. p. 2, 7, 8, 32, 48, 52; Jose Rubio p. 2, 14, 16, 31, 39, 42, 43, 64, 65, 66, 69; David Shephard (Bright Agency) p. 24, 26, 44; Sean Tiffany p. 9, 11, 18, 25, 29, 40, 46, 62, 70, 71, 80; Laszlo Veres (Beehive Illustration) p. 68.

Video Stills:

Discovery Communications, LLC 2015: pages 72, 73, 74, 76, 77, 78, 81, 82, 83, 84, 85, 86, 87, 88, 89, 90, & 91.

Notes

Notes

Notes

Notes

Notes